CONTENTS

Volume 2:   Exodus—Deuteronomy   by Rebecca Abts Wright

Art and Photo Credits: p. 16, Victoria & Albert Museum, London/Art Resource, NY; p. 41, Alinari/Art Resource, NY.

INTRODUCTION TO THE SERIES

The leader's guides provided for use with JOURNEY THROUGH THE BIBLE make the following assumptions:

- adults learn in different ways:
  - —by reading
  - —by listening to speakers
  - —by working on projects
  - —by drama and roleplay
  - —by using their imaginations
  - —by expressing themselves creatively
  - —by teaching others
- the mix of persons in your group is different from that found in any other group;
- the length of the actual time you have for teaching in a session may vary from thirty minutes to ninety minutes;
- the physical place where your class meets is not exactly like the place where any other group or class meets;
- your teaching skills, experiences, and preferences are unlike anyone else's.

We encourage you to discover and develop the ways you can best use the information and learning ideas in this leader's guide with your particular class. To get started, we suggest you try following these steps:

1. Think and pray about your individual class members. Who are they? What are they like? Why are they involved in this particular Bible study class at this particular time in their lives? What seem to be their needs? How do you think they learn best?
2. Think and pray about your class members as a group. A group takes on a character that can be different from the particular characters of the individuals who make up that group. How do your class members interact? What do they enjoy doing together? What would help them become stronger as a group?
3. Keep in mind that you are teaching this class for the sake of the class members, in order to help them increase in their faithfulness as disciples of Jesus Christ. Teachers sometimes fall prey to the danger of teaching in ways that are easiest for themselves. The best teachers accept the discomfort of taking risks and stretching their teaching skills in order to focus on what will really help the class members learn and grow in their faith.
4. Read the chapter in the study book. Read the assigned Bible passages. Read the background Bible passages, if any. Work through the Dimension 1 questions in the study book. Make a list of any items you do not understand and need to research further using such tools as Bible dictionaries, concordances, Bible atlases, and com-

mentaries. In other words, do your homework. Be prepared with your own knowledge about the Bible passages being studied by your class.

5. Read the chapter's material in the leader's guide. You might want to begin with the "Additional Bible Helps," found at the *end* of each chapter. Then look at each learning idea in the "Learning Menu."
6. Spend some time with the "Learning Menu." Notice that the "Learning Menu" is organized around Dimensions 1, 2, and 3 in the study book. Recognizing that different adults and adult classes will learn best using different teaching/learning methods, in each of the three dimensions try to find
   - —at least one learning idea that is primarily discussion-based;
   - —at least one learning idea that begins with a method other than discussion, but which may lead into discussion.

   Make notes about which learning ideas will work best given the unique makeup and setting of your class.
7. Decide on a lesson plan: Which learning ideas will you lead the class members through when? What materials will you need? What other preparations do you need to make? How long do you plan to spend on a particular learning idea?
8. Many experienced teachers have found that they do better if they plan more than they actually use during a class session. They also know that their class members may become frustrated if they try to do too much during a class session. In other words
   - —plan more than you can actually use. That way, you have back-up learning ideas in case something does not work well or something takes much less time than you thought.
   - —don't try to do everything listed in the "Learning Menu." We have intentionally offered you much more than you can use in one class session.
   - —be flexible while you teach. A good lesson plan is only a guide for your use as you teach people. Keep the focus on your class members, not your lesson plan.
9. After you teach, evaluate the class session. What worked well? What did not? What did you learn from your experience of teaching that will help you plan for the next class session?

May God's Spirit be upon you as you lead your class on their *Journey Through the Bible*!

Questions or comments?
Call Curric-U-Phone 1-800-251-8591.

1

Exodus 1:1–2:25

SETTING THE SCENE

LEARNING MENU

Keeping in mind the ways your class members learn best, as well as their needs and interests, choose at least one learning segment from each of the three Dimensions.

Dimension 1:
What Does the Bible Say?

Some of the Dimension 1 questions in the study book will have answers that can easily be recognized directly from the biblical text. Others will involve interpretation and may result in more than one response from class members.

(A) Answer the questions in the study book.

Although answers to Dimension 1 questions will grow out of the specifics of the text itself, at least sometimes they should lead class members to make connections with other texts and with their own lives.

1. Pharaoh sees how the Israelites are growing "more numerous and more powerful than we." He fears that if a war breaks out the Israelites will fight against the Egyptians, joining their enemies.
2. Pharaoh enslaves the Israelites, forcing them to perform hard labor. He also commands that no Israelite baby boys should be allowed to live.
3. The Hebrew midwives "feared God" and let the baby boys live.
4. The question about who has the most power in these chapters may lead to discussion, first, of what constitutes "power" and how it is measured. One important point to remember is that if persons have power they are able to achieve their purposes. Is the frustrated king really more powerful than the lowly midwives who successfully block his intent to destroy the baby Hebrew boys?

(B) Read Pharaoh's speeches.

- Ask for volunteers to read aloud Pharaoh's speeches in Exodus 1. To whom are the words in verses 9-10 spoken? in what manner? with what response from his listeners? Ask other class members to act out various responses.

- Verses 16 and 18 are spoken to the midwives, with their disobedience noted in verse 17. Would Pharaoh speak the same way each time? What are some other ways the women might have responded to what they were told in verse 16?

Dimension 2: What Does the Bible Mean?

(C) Look for hinges.

Exodus 1:1-6 is called a "hinge" between Genesis and Exodus. There are many references throughout Exodus to stories from Genesis.

- Ask the class members to be alert in their reading for things that seem to be "echoes" of some of the material in Genesis.

(D) Review events in Genesis 37–50.

- Ask class members to help you reconstruct a brief review of the events that preceded the words of Exodus 1:5b: "Joseph was already in Egypt." List these events on a chalkboard, marker board, or sheet of newsprint.

(E) Do a word study.

"And a new king arose over Egypt, who did not know Joseph." This is an important verse, in part because of the several levels of the word "know" (*yada*). This notion of a biblical word's having multiple meanings may be new to some class members.

- Write the word *run* on the chalkboard, marker board, or on a large piece of newsprint where everyone can see it easily.
- Ask, "Who knows what this word means?" See how many different definitions the class members can come up with, writing each for all to see. These definitions may range from a hole in a woman's stocking to a small stream (my first parish included Cherry Run United Methodist Church) to being a candidate for elective office.

  All human languages seem to have this feature. Some words have many meanings, some of them nuances of a basic definition and others seemingly unrelated to one another. In one's native language one learns to sort out the intended meanings from the context of the surrounding words. The process happens so quickly and automatically that it is done without conscious thought.

- Write, "The Tigers made one run in the first inning." Below that sentence write, "Tigers run to catch their prey."

  Nobody native to the English language would be likely to confuse the meanings of *run* in these sentences. What we need to be aware of in Bible study is that neither biblical Hebrew nor biblical Greek is our native language. Thus we will have to do consciously and deliberately what in English (or Korean or Spanish or whatever language we learned first) happens automatically.

The Bible is full of instances where specific words have been used, apparently because of their particular nuances that may not come through in translation. Many of these will be noted either in the study book or in this leader's guide under the "Additional Bible Helps," toward the end of each chapter. Not only may seeing these additional meanings help the significance of a passage to become clearer, it can also add to our delight on a purely aesthetic level.

(F) Compare words *basket* and *ark*.

- Call attention to the study book explanation of the words *basket, ark, chalice,* and *goblet* (page 6). Ask students to think of other words that may "mean" the same thing but "feel" different. List them where everyone can see these words.

(G) Consider where God is when God is not mentioned.

- Discuss why God is not mentioned in the story of the infant Moses' rescue. Indeed, everything proceeds "naturally," with no hint of miracle or any sort of divine intervention. Yet the writer seems to be sensing the mystery of God's providence through the human actors and their deeds. Ask class members for examples of how God's actions can be discerned in ordinary events today.

(H) Dramatize Exodus 2:12a.

- Ask class members to pair off to read this half-verse, one of each pair adding a "stage direction" and the other putting in what Moses might have been saying to himself. For example:
  Person A: He looks frantically, first to the left, then to the right.

  Person B: "Where is a policeman when you need him?"

- After the pairs have spent a few minutes on this activity, ask for volunteers to share their renditions with the entire class. Then ask class members what insights they have gained about any difference it makes to what follows, both in the verse and in the rest of the story.

(I) Roleplay Exodus 2:15b-21.

- If class members are comfortable with roleplaying, ask them to act out this section. The point here is to see how whole realms of meaning may come through from different tones of voice. Flat words on a page are enlivened when class members try to put themselves into the biblical roles. Here are some examples:

Will the seven daughters seem as afraid of Moses as they had been of the shepherds? (After all, to them he is a foreigner, an Egyptian; on the other hand, he has done them an unexpected kindness.)

Is Moses fearful? Does he show the effects of the fear resulting from his narrow escape from Pharaoh?

How eager are Reuel's daughters to have this stranger accept their father's invitation to "break bread"?

And so forth.

(J) Consider the many roles Moses had to fulfill by Exodus 2:22.

● How many different identities has Moses had? In small groups ask class members to list them. Give an example or two, such as:

—Three months as a hidden Hebrew infant;

—Somewhere between two and six years, approximately, as a princess's Hebrew "foster child";

—Perhaps twenty to thirty years as an Egyptian in Pharaoh's court;

—A Hebrew who observes hard-working slaves and identifies with them as his "kinfolk";

—An Egyptian who helps seven Midianite girls;

—A husband and father in a Midianite family.

● In small groups, discuss these identities. Ask, "Which one is the 'real' Moses? Why did you make that choice?"

● Ask groups to report back to whole class.

(K) Compare expectations and realities.

● Ask two class members to read aloud the following assumptions and realities that underlie Exodus 1–2:

Assumption: important people are identified by their names; the unimportant go nameless.

Reality (in this section of Exodus): the ruler and his daughter are unnamed; two mere midwives are specified by name.

Assumption: our people are the "good guys"; the "bad guys" are foreigners.

Reality: Moses and his family are on "our side." But so are Pharaoh's daughter and the Midianite priest and his shepherd daughters (foreigners). Pharaoh, the Egyptian overseer, and the other Midianite shepherds are "bad guys," but so is the Hebrew who is beating up his fellow Hebrew.

(L) Chart examples of oppression.

● Write the following chart on chalkboard, marker board, or newsprint where everyone can see it; leave two columns at right to be filled in later.

OPPRESSOR	OPPRESSED		
Egyptian	Hebrew		
Hebrew	Hebrew		
Midianites	Midianites (sisters)		

● Ask for comments and questions, then add the third column and the heading only to the last column. Ask the whole class to fill in the last column.

OPPRESSOR	OPPRESSED	MOSES' ACTION	RESULT
Egyptian	Hebrew	Beating	
Hebrew	Hebrew	Talking	
Midianites	Midianites	Helped sisters	

Dimension 3: What Does the Bible Mean to Us?

(M) Consider what makes class members who they are.

● Ask class members to share identity-sayings they grew up with. Perhaps such expressions were general, such as "Boys don't cry" or "Little ladies mustn't shout." Maybe there are some specific to families: "A Bradford would never _____." Did they as children believe these sayings were true? Do they now?

● Why does the taunt some siblings throw at each other— "You're adopted!"—have such power?

● If some in the class are parents, can they think of any such sayings they are passing on to their own children?

● Such identity questions also play a role in larger groups. Ask for stereotypes about poor people compared to rich people. Also consider people who live in the country in contrast to city dwellers. How about "Southern hospitality" or "urban rudeness"?

● If your class has the good fortune of including more than one ethnic group, perhaps persons from different ethnic backgrounds would be willing to share how and under what circumstances they feel the-same-as or different-from members of other groups.

● What about the identities "Christian" and "American"?

—Are these identities identical?

—If they differ, where are the contrasts?
—Are there ever conflicts? If so, how are they resolved?

(N) Read a chapter aloud.

- Walt Harrington's book *Crossings: A White Man's Journey into Black America* (HarperCollins, 1993) is the story of a white man, married to an African American woman. For the sake of his children he makes three journeys in different regions of the United States to discover, insofar as any white person could, the state of black/white relations today. The chapters are reports of his conversations and observations. If you can get this book, read aloud one of the short chapters as a starting point for discussion.

(O) Discuss the power of names.

- Ask for responses to the holiday greeting card mentioned in the study book (page 9). Have others had similar experiences? Perhaps some persons have been called by their first names by physicians or other professionals who refer to themselves by title and surname. Does such a practice really make a difference? For whom?

- What about nicknames? Sometimes they are a source of embarrassment; other times they are a badge of belonging. Ask class members, "If you could make your name anything at all, what would it be? Why?"

- Ask class members how they would like to be addressed within this particular class.

(P) Consider fate, luck, and God's providence.

- Ask class members their feelings about Christians wishing one another "Good luck!"

- In small groups ask them to come up with some other greeting that conveys the speaker's good wishes without invoking the concept of "luck."

  Some in the class may say that "Good luck!" isn't non-Christian, that it is just an expression. This could lead into the discussion of words and what they mean or do not mean as we use them in different contexts, as previously noted in activity "E" (Tiger runs; tigers run).

(Q) Contrast wisdom and foolishness.

- Jesus and Paul both have things to say about the relationship of wisdom and foolishness. In small groups look at Matthew 11:25 as well as 1 Corinthians 1:18-31 and 3:18-20. Ask small groups to discuss whether the wisdom and foolishness being contrasted in those passages bears any relationship to the "shrewd dealings" of

Pharaoh and the Egyptians in Exodus 1. If so, how are they similar or dissimilar?

- Allow time for groups to report their findings.

(R) Compare two Bible stories of fragile beginnings of our faith.

- In small groups compare Exodus 2:1-10 with Matthew 2:1-18.

- Why do you think that when the story of the Wise Men in Matthew 2 is used in Sunday school or worship services verses 16-18 are often omitted?

- Read a quotation to the whole class. Ask for their response to it in light of this comparison:

  "The grim reality is that even when redemption finally comes, it is accompanied, not by the heroic martyrdom of the brave partisan, but by the senseless murder of children. The salvation promised by God is not greeted by a waiting world, but opposed with the hysterical fanaticism which borders on madness" (from *The Book of Exodus: A Critical Theological Commentary*, by Brevard S. Childs; Westminster, 1974; page 25).

(S) Roleplay Moses.

Note: If you have done activity "I" you may not want to use this somewhat similar learning activity.

- Dramatize the way Moses responds to three instances of injustice (Egyptian beating Hebrew; Hebrew beating Hebrew; Midianite shepherds stealing water from other Midianites). Point out that technical legal terminology ("who made you ruler and judge over us?") is used when Moses encounters the two Hebrews. Moses has more than a sentimental help-the-underdog feeling toward the Hebrews. Ethnicity may be stronger than upbringing. Or is a sense of fairness stronger still?

- Ask class members to pair off and try reading to their partner in as many tones of voice as they can think of to explain why in Exodus 2:12 Moses "looked this way and that." What do they think he was looking for?

- Then discuss whether you think Moses meant to kill the Egyptian. Did Moses commit murder? first degree murder? "merely" manslaughter? Does his motivation in verse 12a affect how you interpret the rest of this verse?

- Come back as a whole class. Ask for two or three pairs to present their roleplay to the class.

(T) Examine the significance of the marriage of Moses and Zipporah.

- Ask class members to mention words or phrases that could have described Moses and/or Zipporah at each step along the way from their first glimpse of each other to their wedding feast. Write them on chalkboard, marker board, or newsprint.

- Point out that from the very beginning there has been no "pure" bloodline in Israel or elsewhere in the Middle East. "Outsiders" are integrated into the most intimate relationships of the community, even by the leaders.

Additional Bible Helps

Special Words
Exodus 2:2: The word used for the mother's hiding the baby for three months means a particular kind of hiding. It is "treasuring" or "storing up."

Exodus 2:3 and 2:5: The "reeds" where the infant Moses was hidden and the Sea of Reeds through which Moses and God will lead the Israelites to freedom in chapter 14 use the same Hebrew word.

Four verbs in Exodus 2:24-25: Differing translations in the New Revised Standard Version are in **bold type**.

—Hear (*shama'*): Not just to be aware of sounds, but to take heed, to respond. (God **heard**; **observed** [Exodus 3:7]; **given heed to** [Genesis 16:11]; **taken heed of** [Psalm 31:7].)

—Remember (*zaqar*): God is not a kindly, but somewhat forgetful, old uncle whose memory has to be jogged from time to time. As *hearing* is more than just being aware of sounds, so *remembering* is more than calling things to mind. To remember in this sense is to be actively attentive, to be involved. When the text says "God remembered" we have an indication that soon God will act. (God **remembered**.)

—See (*ra'ah*): Again, this is not mere awareness of visual stimuli. It includes understanding ("Oh yes, I see") and sympathetic involvement. (In Exodus 2:11 Moses *saw* the forced labor oppressing his fellow Hebrews and *saw* the Egyptian beating the Hebrew.) (God **looked upon**.)

—Know (*yada*): This verb is the same verb as used in Exodus 1:8. (See the discussion in the study book, pages 4–5.) God is here contrasted with Pharaoh, who did not know. (God **took notice**.)

Use of any of these verbs with God as the subject would bring a powerful message to the original audience. The combination of all four, especially with the repetition of the subject "God" each time (instead of using a pronoun) alerts everyone that something is going to happen. God is going to act.

On Sameness and Differentness Among People
The Creation account in Genesis 1 (King James Version) makes repeated mention of each plant or animal being created "after its kind" (Genesis 1:11, 12, 21, 24, 25). How-ever, with the creation of human beings, there is no mention of "kind," either in Chapter 1 or in Chapter 2's version. To be sure, marriage with Canaanites and others in the land when Israel arrives is frequently forbidden. The reasons given, however, are theological. The concern has nothing to do with bloodlines or "genetic purity" but rather with the avoidance of idolatry. If your sons marry their daughters, the people are warned, those women "will make your sons also prostitute themselves to their gods" (Exodus 34:16b). On the other side, many Israelites from patriarchs through kings and commoners did take non-Israelite wives. A signal example is Ruth of Moab, who is presented as the great-grandmother of King David.

Quotations for pondering

- "In a real sense, the issue at stake is the understanding of the nature of [human] decision for God. Seen from one perspective, the issue is . . . unequivocal in its character, the clear call to discipleship. In another sense, it is a living and deciding among the variety of relations in which we live, seeking in the complexity of mixed sinful emotions and historical accidents to live an obedient life. The selfless act is soon beclouded by violence and nothing of lasting effect is accomplished for Israel's plight. . . . [T]he witness of both testaments to Moses remains in the tension and points to [people's] continuing obligation of wrestling with the decision of faith in the context of a multitude of small decisions of living" (from *The Book of Exodus: A Critical Theological Commentary*, page 43).

- "God uses the weak, what is low and despised in the world, to shame the strong (cf. Jer. 9:23; I Cor. 1:26-29). Rather than using power as it is usually exercised in the world, *God works through persons who have no obvious power*; indeed, they are unlikely candidates for the exercise of power. The choice of the five women in chapters 1—2 entails much risk and vulnerability for God; that risk is real, for these persons could fail and God would have to begin again. But they prove highly effective against the ruthless forms of systemic power" (from *Exodus: Interpretation: A Bible Commentary for Teaching and Preaching*, by Terence E. Fretheim; John Knox Press, 1991; page 37. Emphasis in original).

- "Oppression is the prevailing theme in this unit. Those who live in affluence and freedom will have difficulty understanding the true nature of this experience" (from *Exodus: Interpretation: A Bible Commentary for Teaching and Preaching*; page 29).

2

Exodus 3:1-17a

GOD'S CALL— INITIAL REACTIONS

LEARNING MENU

Keeping in mind the ways your class members learn best, as well as their needs and interests, choose at least one learning segment from each of the three Dimensions.

Dimension 1:
What Does the Bible Say?

(A) Consider possible answers to Dimension 1 questions.

In the study book class members may already have written answers to the five questions on pages 12–13. They may wish to compare their answers with one another, or with the following possibilities:

1. Moses reluctantly accepts God's commission. God shows patience and persistence in convincing Moses to do God's bidding. Moses appears timid, perhaps just fearful of returning to Egypt where he is still wanted for murder. God offers to find a spokesperson to assist Moses.
2. Some of the reasons Moses seems convinced that it is actually God speaking to him might be: the bush that is not consumed; the authoritative voice he hears; the holiness of the place; and, God's self-identification as the "God of Abraham, the God of Isaac, and the God of Jacob."
3. The Israelites were probably eager for any help in their situation. To have the help come from the God of their ancestors added credibility to the words Aaron and Moses told them.
4. Pharaoh dismisses Moses and Aaron as if they were pesky insects. "I do not know your Lord; so go away, stop bothering me," was his message. Then he punished the people for their request to go into the wilderness.
5. Moses has become bolder; he speaks up to God and demands answers from God.

(B) Act out Exodus 3:1-17a.

● Ask for two volunteers to present in dialogue the scene in Exodus 3:1-17a. Here are some starter questions for both the "actors" and the "audience" to have in mind:

1. How might Moses feel in Exodus 3:1? bored? lonely?
2. With what tone of voice does God call Moses' name in verse 4? Is it authoritative? enticing?
3. Why was Moses so afraid in verse 6 that he hid his face?

(C) Imagine receiving a message from God.

- In groups of three to five, discuss what the Israelites in Exodus 4:31 believe, and why? Was it the message or the signs (4:27-30) that caught their attention?

- Allow time for groups to report their findings.

(D) Get into the mind of Pharaoh.

- Divide the class members into two groups or, if you have a large class, an even number of small groups. Ask one group (or half the groups) to discuss Pharaoh's justification for refusing to let the people go as seen from Pharaoh's point of view (Exodus 5:2, 5). Ask the other group (or other half of the groups) to discuss his justification from Moses and Aaron's point of view.

- Background information: It was not unheard of for groups to be allowed time off to participate in religious ceremonies or festivals. That is, what Moses and Aaron asked was not in and of itself unreasonable.

- Let groups report on their discussion.

(E) Read Moses' words.

- Ask for a volunteer to read aloud Moses' words in Exodus 5:22-23.

- How have things changed for Moses since Exodus 3?

Dimension 2: What Does the Bible Mean?

(F) Explore nonverbal messages.

"Remove the sandals from your feet, for the place on which you are standing is holy ground" (Exodus 3:5). Cultural details often carry important meanings. This is no problem unless the detail recounted has no meaning, or a different meaning, in the new culture in which it is narrated. When Moses is told by God to take off his shoes it is at least a sign of respect, even more a sign of servanthood, or going so far as to signify slavery. "Egyptian custom required going barefoot in the presence of a superior, especially the king" (from *Exploring Exodus: The Heritage of Biblical Israel*, by Nahum M. Sarna; Schocken Books, 1986; page 40).

- Ask class members to give examples of clothing that conveys symbolic meaning.

—For a man to remove his hat inside a building is a gesture of respect.

—It formerly was considered a gesture of respect for a woman to put on a hat for attending church services.

Particular social customs differ, but their meanings are similar: particular clothing and gestures are used to convey honor; particular items are worn in certain circumstances and removed in others.

(G) Examine the meaning of some biblical clothes.

- As a whole group list other biblical instances when clothing carries particular meaning. To "prime the pump" you might mention:

—Joseph's special robe (Genesis 37);

—The robe and shoes called for at the prodigal son's return (Luke 15).

The prodigal son's garments would have had similar sorts of meanings to Joseph's robe and Moses' shoes. Jesus' audience listening to this parable would have known "without thinking about it" that this younger son was not going to be treated by his father like a slave or even a hired servant. He was being welcomed back into the family, taking up the same place he had earlier abandoned, acknowledged by his father as still a son.

(H) Sample the activity called "form criticism."

- Before class time, write two lists on the board or newsprint:

A	B
Once upon a time	Sincerely yours,
2 cups flour	Yours forever and a day,
Dear Mr. Perkins:	Serves 6
My Dearest Darling Snookums,	And they lived happily ever after.

- With the whole group together, match each opening in the first column with the most appropriate closing in the second column.

- Then ask class members to describe the kind of message that would go between each pair.

Knowing what things "fit" with one another and what style would likely come within them is included in the Bible-study technique known as "Form Criticism." The shape or form of a passage gives certain clues to its content.

One example of a "form" is the Prophetic Call Narrative. It has five basic parts. Write these parts on chalkboard, marker board, or newsprint for everyone to see:

Setting
God's appearing/getting one's attention
Task
Objection
Response

"Once upon a time . . . and they lived happily ever after" identifies the form "Fairy Tale" in which we should not be surprised to meet talking frogs or magic wands. Similarly, the form of the Prophetic Call Narrative would have alerted the early hearers of Exodus that Moses was being called by God to perform a particular task. It would not have been necessary to say that in so many words; the form said it.

● In groups of two to four, ask class members to identify the five elements of the Prophetic Call Narrative form in Exodus 3:1-16.

● Then ask half the groups to read Judges 6 and half the groups Luke 1 to see another example of the Prophetic Call Narrative. What do these Scriptures tell us about Gideon or Mary?

● Allow time for groups to report their findings.

(I) Write an answer from God.

● Divide class members into groups of two to four.

● Ask each group to read Moses' questions in Exodus 5:22-23. Let them try asking the questions of one another in different tones of voice: whining, demanding, and so forth.

● Next ask each group to compose an answer from God to Moses and title it "Exodus 5:24."

● Let the groups share their responses by having one group member read Moses' words in verses 22-23 and another read God's reply. What tone of voice would God use in reply?

Dimension 3:
What Does the Bible Mean to Us?

(J) Ask for class responses to study book.

● See if any class members wish to discuss the questions and issues raised in the study book under Dimension 3. Some may wish to give an example from their own experience of a time when some people saw evidence of God's presence and others did not.

(K) Look for symbols of God's presence.

● Exodus 3 uses the figure of fire to stand for the presence of God. As a whole group list what other symbols for God's presence you can find in your classroom or sanctuary.

(L) Create symbols.

● You will need paper and crayons or markers for everyone to use.

● Divide class members into groups of three or four to make a visual, nonverbal symbol of God's presence. Before letting the groups explain their own creations, let the whole class look at them all, with volunteers saying what they see and feel from the works of other groups.

(M) Suggest a name for God.

"YHWH" stands for God's personal name. God's name is not "God," nor is it "Lord." *God* is more like a job description; *Lord* is a title. It may be difficult to think of God not having a name in the same way we have names.

● In small groups ask the class members to suggest names for God.

Many suggestions (Lord, Almighty, King of kings) may be titles rather than names. Press class members to see if they can come up with a personal name, or even something we might call a "nickname." (You might mention the legendary confusion of a small child: "Harold be thy name.")

One difficulty could be that some class members may feel it disrespectful to think of God's having something as trivial as a nickname. Others may be disturbed by the thought of using a name such as "John" or "Jane," because those are identified in this culture as masculine and feminine names. And, as a current sweatshirt message says, " 'God' is not a boy's name." Still, for every class that has members not wanting to give God a boy's name, there will be others distressed at the slightest hint that this activity encourages them to call God by a girl's name. After all, didn't Jesus himself call God "Father"? Yes, of course. However, that is another example, not of a name, but of a title.

Maybe someone will suggest "Leslie" or "Jean" or "Sidney" or something similar—names that do not unambiguously designate gender.

● Read the portion of William Raspberry's column from *The Washington Post* (November 29, 1993) in the study book, page 20. Do his words give any guidance in choosing a name for God?

(N) Consider ways we feel God's presence.

- Ask the class members to list times they have felt the presence of God in a special way.
- In pairs ask class members to tell one another what helped them know it was God.

(O) Discuss everyday sayings.

- Write the following sayings on the board or newsprint before class. Feel free to add other similar ones. Leave some blank space for the class members' additions.
—"To make an omelet, you have to break some eggs."
—"It's always darkest just before the dawn."
—"All's fair in love and war."
- Ask for reactions from class members to such sayings.
—Are they true?
—Are they adequate maxims for Christians?
- Ask class members to make connections between such sayings and Exodus 5.

(P) Consider if God plays fair.

- In light of Exodus 5:9, why should the Israelites listen to Moses and Aaron again?
- In light of 5:22, why should Moses listen to YHWH (the LORD) again?

    Here is an arena in which the Bible is totally honest. In a fallen world, God's will is not always done. Sometimes things seem to be getting worse instead of better.

(Q) Learn about your pastor's call to ministry.

- Invite the pastor of your church to come to your class to discuss God's "call." Some questions you might want to ask may include these:
—How did you know it was God?
—How did you know what God wanted you to do?
—Did you ask any questions or raise any objections as Moses did?
—Does God call people to do tasks that do not require them to be ordained? If so, how can we know when we are called?

(R) Read some midrashim.

- Midrashim (mid-RASH-im; plural of midrash) are Jewish commentaries on the Hebrew Scriptures collected between A.D. 400 and 1200. Read, or have a class member read, these two midrashim about Moses and the burning bush. (The Hebrew word translated "bush" refers to a bramble or a thorny bush.)
- "A heathen asked R[abbi] Joshua ben Korhah: Why did the Holy One see fit to speak to Moses out of a thorn-bush and not out of another kind of tree? He replied: Had he spoken to Moses out of a carob tree or out of a sycamore tree, you would have asked me the same question; but to dismiss you with no reply is not right. So I will tell you why. To teach you that no place on earth, not even a thornbush, is devoid of the Presence" (quoted in *The Book of Legends: Sefer Ha-Aggadah*, edited by Hayim Nahman Bialik and Yehoshua Hana Ravnitzky, translated by William G. Braude; Schocken Books, 1992; page 63).
- "Another comment: 'Out of the midst of a thornbush.' R[abbi] Yose said: Why out of a thornbush? It is characteristic of a thornbush that when a man sticks his hand into it, he is not injured, because the sharp ends of its thorns are pointed downward; but when he attempts to draw his hand out of the bush, the thorns will fasten on to it. Likewise, when the Israelites first entered Egypt, they were well received, being told, 'The land of Egypt is open before thee; in the best of the land make thy father and thy brethren to dwell' (Gen. 47:6). But when they wanted to leave, the Egyptians fastened on to them, as when Pharaoh said, 'I will not let Israel go' (Exodus 5:2)" (quoted in *The Book of Legends*; pages 62–63).

(S) End with a time of reflection.

- About five minutes before the end of the class period, ask each person to reflect on what has gone on during the hour. Go around the room, and ask each person to say one thing he or she will ponder during the coming week.

Additional Bible Helps

Word Study

We do not expect that the persons using this study series are linguists or have any interest in becoming Hebrew scholars. Neither can we pretend that some important theological issues are not intertwined in issues of language and the sorry fact that, as John Ciardi aptly put it, "Translation is the art of the best possible failure."

Biblical Hebrew was written originally with consonants only. Vowels are necessary, of course, for pronunciation. When only a few people could read and write they knew what vowels to insert. To this day, Torah scrolls used in Jewish synagogues are written without vowels or chanting signs. The readers must learn not only which vowels go in which words, but also which notes are used for each syllable. Writing nothing but consonants makes for great economy of space, but can also make for ambiguity in reading. The context usually removes the ambiguity.

Filling in the necessary vowels is not a skill limited to rabbis or scholars. You may wish to try this activity with your class members:

a. Write "Mr." and "Mrs." on the board or newsprint.

b. Ask a volunteer to read what you wrote.

c. Ask how that person knew what to say.

The abbreviations *Mr.* and *Mrs.*, like *bvsplsk*, are impossible to pronounce. People learn what abbreviations are "supposed" to sound like and, with practice, do not have to go through a long mental process. One sees *Mr.* and automatically says *mister*.

Potentially ambiguous forms do not always give trouble, especially when in context.

a. Write *St.*

b. Ask someone to read what you wrote. (Probably you will get both *saint* and *street* as answers. If not, supply the missing term!)

c. Write *St. John* and *John St.*

d. Ask if class members now know what to say for each *St.*

God's Name

What God gives to Moses, as represented in the Hebrew text, is nothing but consonants, put into our alphabet as YHWH. In part because of the commandment not to misuse God's name, the practice grew up of never saying the name at all. But something has to be said when coming to "YHWH" in the text. The traditional solution was to put the vowels for "the name" with the consonants for God's personal name; and when one comes to that word in the Hebrew text, one says "Adonai" (AD-oh-nigh), meaning "Lord." In many English translations this is signaled by the use of small caps "LORD," to differentiate it from those places where the actual word "Lord" occurs.

What about *Jehovah*? *Jehovah* is a hybrid word that comes from the German-language transliteration of God's consonants with their inserted vowels. A German *J* has the English sound of our *Y*; a German *V* corresponds to an English *W*. What about using *Yahweh*, as some translations such as *The Jerusalem Bible* do? This is the best guess of some scholars as to how the name sounded originally. In view of the tradition NOT to pronounce the name, many people still prefer not to pronounce it. This book follows the New Revised Standard Version (NRSV) practice of using "LORD." It is important to remind students from time to time that "LORD" (with small caps) represents a name—like Ted or Jane—and not a title.

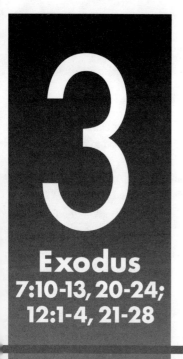

3

Exodus
7:10-13, 20-24;
12:1-4, 21-28

WORSE
BEFORE
BETTER

LEARNING MENU

Keeping in mind the ways your class members learn best, as well as their needs and interests, choose at least one learning segment from each of the three Dimensions.

Dimension 1:
What Does the Bible Say?

(A) Answer the questions in the study book.

1. "The magicians of Egypt" perform the same signs that Moses and Aaron perform before Pharaoh.
2. Again the Egyptian magicians are able to duplicate the sign performed by Aaron and Moses, so Pharaoh pays no attention to Aaron and Moses.
3. Each Israelite family (or group of small families) is to slaughter a lamb and place some of its blood on their doorpost. Then "none of you shall go outside the door of your house until morning."
4. The people are told to "keep this observance" by regularly telling their children about how the LORD "passed over" the Israelite homes while killing the first-born of the Egyptians and how the LORD led them out of slavery.

(B) Roleplay two scenes.

● Ask for volunteers to act out the scenes in Exodus 7:10-13, 20-24. You will need MOSES, AARON, PHARAOH, COURT MAGICIANS, and NARRATOR. Give them a short time to prepare their roleplay.

● Ask for more volunteers to roleplay MOSES and the ISRAELITES when the instructions for Passover are given (Exodus 12:1-4, 21-22).
—What more would the people like to know?
—Has anything been left out?

Dimension 2:
What Does the Bible Mean?

(C) Think of possible tabloid headlines concerning the Bible.

● From time to time a supermarket tabloid will have a cover story about the finding of some "proof" for one or another biblical story. Make up some "headlines" and have them displayed in the room before class time. Use your imagination; it would be hard to come up with anything wilder than some already published!

—Assume that at least some of these findings were true. What effect would that have on your Christian faith?
—Assume that a particular Bible story were proved to be false. Would that have any effect on your faith?

Sun • Vol. 10, No. 8 • February 25, 1992

"Two broken stone tablets inscribed with the
TEN COMMANDMENTS FOUND
Gulf war bombs opened a hidden cavern that held the word of God"

Sun • Vol. 12, No. 18 • May 3, 1994

"MOSES' GRAVE FOUND AT MT. SINAI
Stone tablet proves he's ancient leader who defeated evil pharaoh"

Weekly World News • June 2, 1992

"The Bible's Garden of Eden Discovered South of Denver!
ADAM & EVE'S SKELETONS FOUND—
IN COLORADO!
Amazing proof Book of Genesis is true!"

(D) Discuss what constitutes an act of God.

Exodus 8:18-19: We tend to refer to things that seem to be outside our control as miracles. A good example is the magicians being unable to conjure up gnats. They explained this failure by claiming that what Moses and Aaron were doing was by the power of God.

What constitutes an act of God? Does it have to be something that is impossible by human understanding? Sometimes we seem to see God's action better after the fact. Looking back, pondering an event, we may say, "God did indeed have a hand in that."

● Ask for class members to share examples of miracles or acts of God from their own life.

(E) Talk about biblical signs.

The study book says, "Pharaoh's magicians are able to duplicate the first three of the signs (rod to snake; water to blood; frogs). They try to make gnats but cannot. As long as they could do the same things as Aaron and Moses, we are told that Pharaoh's heart remained hardened (7:22)."

● Discuss the questions in the study book in the first part of Dimension 3, page 26.

● Ask the class members to think of times when competing groups seem to be making persons' lives worse rather than better.

● In international peace talks, is the issue who has the most weapons, or is the issue stable peace?

● "Signs" today in domestic politics seem to be in the form of popularity polls. Bring an example from a local political race.

—Does the fact that a particular slogan wins support make it right?
—What are our options, other than "dropping out" altogether or becoming cynical? Sometimes someone is needed to break the old cycle.

(F) Take another look at "providence" and "luck."

● Look again at the last chapter's discussion of the relationship of providence and luck. Talk about the following:

—How does one see God at work in the world?
—Is God recognized only in things that are otherwise inexplicable?

(G) Make plans for passing our tradition on to children.

● In groups of three or four find out how your congregation passes on the Christian faith and your church's traditions to its children.

● How do we include our own children? other children within our church? What about children whose families have no connection with any church?

● What specific thing can your class do to pass on your Christian faith to your children, grandchildren, nieces and nephews, and other children of the church?

(H) Find out more about miracles.

Chapter 2 (page 13 in the study book) pointed out both that the miracle of the burning bush fades into the background almost immediately and that God's self-identifying is tied less to the supernatural than to specific history and specific interactions with specific people. This is a persistent biblical theme.

—God acts, and God acts in human history.

—God speaks, not in "timeless truths" that hover somewhere in the middle distance, but to flesh-and-blood human beings. This is in no way to discount the miracles that are reported. It is to warn, however, lest we be another "faithless generation" looking only for such signs.

● Divide the class members into four groups. Ask each group look up one of the following passages:

—Luke 11:29-32

—Matthew 12:38-42

—Matthew 16:1-4

—Mark 8:11-12

● Ask the groups to study their passages with the following questions in mind:

—What is the relationship between signs and faith?

—Were the court magicians correct in seeing God acting in those signs that they could not duplicate?

(I) Consider how God responds to persons—even opponents—who heed God's message.

Beginning with the fourth plague, a distinction is made between the Israelites and the Egyptians. Exodus 9:19-21 shows that God often makes distinctions. Some of the Egyptians "feared the word of the LORD" and brought their slaves and their livestock to safety while others suffered the consequences of the immense hailstones.

● Ask the class members

—What groups could be described as "God's enemies" today? followers of Saddam Hussein? of Castro? members of the KKK? liberals in the church? fundamentalists? atheists?

—What should be the church's response to such groups?

—In groups of three or four, ask persons to compose sentence prayers for specific "enemies of God."

(J) Consider if God can be unfair.

The study book raises the question of God's unfairness in hardening Pharaoh's heart, but does not give an answer that solves all the potential problems (see "Hardening the Heart," pages 24–25).

● Review this section in the study book.

● Ask class members how comfortable they are leaving things in such an open-ended manner.

● Does it seem that God is working against Moses? How would you feel about being a salesperson, knowing that your boss was undermining you by making your customer refuse to consider what you are trying to sell?

(K) Read some quotations to spark discussion.

● "Inevitably the question arises: does God intervene to prevent repentance and obedience to his will and, if so, can the person thus prevented be held guilty for unrepentance and disobedience?" (*The Message of Exodus*, by Lester Meyer; Augsburg, 1983; page 75).

● "Whatever the purpose of the plagues may be, they are not punishment for an innocent monarch being helplessly manipulated by an arbitrary deity" (*The Message of Exodus*, page 77).

● Regarding the innocent bystanders among the general Egyptian population: "In the biblical view, society as a corporate entity cannot evade responsibility for the follies and evils committed in its name, and it cannot escape the consequences thereof. Egypt is about to suffer a concentrated succession of disasters" (from *Exploring Exodus: The Heritage of Biblical Israel*, by Nahum M. Sarna; Schocken Books, 1986; page 68).

—How would you relate such a "biblical view" to our nation?

—to your denomination?

—to your local church?

—to your family?

● In Zora Neale Hurston's novel *Moses: Man of the Mountain*, Aaron and Moses are on their way to see Pharaoh after the plague of frogs.

" 'We fixed him that time,' Aaron gloated on the way. 'I'll bet he wants to tell us he's glad to let us Hebrews go.'

" 'That may be so, Aaron, but I doubt it.'

" 'Why?'

" 'Because, if Pharaoh lets me lead off the Hebrews, he will be driven from his throne by the nobles. They think they can't exist without slaves and Pharaoh wouldn't dare to go against them, not that he wants to anyway' " (University of Illinois Press, 1984; page 195).

● After the plague of flies is removed, and Pharaoh once again goes back on his word, Moses announces the cattle plague, saying, in Hurston's novel:

" 'One thing only can save you—when you come to know that justice is greater than pride. You know where I live when you get ready to talk sense.'

"And Moses walked away.

"Moses walked out of the palace of Pharaoh knowing that he carried Pharaoh's peace and security in his hand.

"If Pharaoh relented and let the Hebrews go, he would rid himself of the worry and humiliation he was suffering. But on the other hand he would have to face a danger more sure and certain right away. The nobles would never permit him to save his face at their expense. Even the servants who served about him personally belonged to that ruling class and so he could not even hope to escape with his life. If the house of Pharaoh had not preached and practiced hatred and vengeance for generations, he could save himself by a show of generosity and dismiss the slaves. But the intolerance of Pharaoh and his fathers was fighting against him. Pharaoh was locked up in his own palace and inside himself" (*Moses: Man of the Mountain*; pages 206–207).

(L) End with a time of reflection.

● About five minutes before the end of the class period, ask each person to reflect on what has gone on during the hour. Go around the room and ask each person to say one thing he or she will ponder during the coming week.

Moses and the Plague of Locusts. German woodcut from the Gutenberg Bible.
Victoria & Albert Museum, London/Art Resource, NY.

Additional Bible Helps

Rationalizing the Plagues

"The 'Plagues of Egypt' are variously designated as 'plagues' (9:14; 12:13); 'signs' (7:3; 8:23; 10:1-2); 'portents' (7:3; 11:9-10); and 'stroke,' 'visitation,' or 'plague' (11:1). In this general context these terms are synonymous; together they are God's 'great acts of judgment' (7:4). . . .

"There have been many efforts to rationalize these fantastic stories. Modern scholars have sought to provide a natural explanation at least for the core of each sign. . . . Thus the fetid river, with its decaying fish, bred a crop of frogs. Whereupon the decomposing frogs caused the swarms of insects in the third and fourth plagues. These again lead to the fifth and sixth plagues. This is a highly dubious and conjectural procedure. More seriously, it causes one to forget the real purpose of the stories in their total context. It betrays a concern for historical veracity or congruity at the cost of meaning and truth. To be sure, many of these stories reflect something of the natural conditions and hazards of life in Egypt. Furthermore, some of them probably rest on actual events that facilitated the escape of the Israelites, and in which they saw the hand of God. But the text now presents a series of piously decorated accounts, woven together in an elaborate and artistic series of narratives. The significance and value of this total complex is symbolic rather than historical. The mosaic as a whole attests Israel's faith, resting on the historic experience of its escape from slavery; it aims at showing that not Pharaoh or the gods of Egypt but the living God of Israel makes nature serve [humankind]—or rather, makes nature serve [God's] purposes for [human] fulfillment" (from *The Interpreter's Bible*, Volume 1; Abingdon, 1952; pages 838–39.)

The Ten Plagues

First Plague	Water Turned to Blood	(Exodus 7:14-24)
Second Plague	Frogs	(Exodus 8:1-15)
Third Plague	Gnats	(Exodus 8:16-19)
Fourth Plague	Flies	(Exodus 8:20-32)
Fifth Plague	Livestock Diseased	(Exodus 9:1-7)
Sixth Plague	Boils	(Exodus 9:8-12)
Seventh Plague	Thunder and Hail	(Exodus 9:13-35)
Eighth Plague	Locusts	(Exodus 10:1-20)
Ninth Plague	Darkness	(Exodus 10:21-29)
Tenth Plague	Death of the First-born	(Exodus 11:1-10; 12:29-32)

4

Exodus 14:5-14, 21-28

GET READY, GET SET, FREE!

Dimension 1:
What Does the Bible Say?

(A) Discuss answers to the questions in Dimension 1 of the study book.

1. God led the Israelites by a longer, less direct route to avoid their being tempted to return to Egypt because that would be easier than to continue on their journey.
2. Pharaoh and his officials were appalled at having let their slaves leave Egypt and immediately roused the army to follow them and bring them back.
3. The Israelites were terrified when they realized the Egyptians were pursuing them. They immediately turned on Moses and on God, accusing them of leading the people to their death in the wilderness.
4. Moses tried to calm the people's fears, telling them to trust in the LORD: "The LORD will fight for you, and you have only to keep still."
5. At the LORD's command Moses raised his hand over the sea, the waters parted, and the Israelites crossed the sea on dry land. As the Egyptian army followed the people into the dry seabed, Moses raised his hand again and the waters returned, drowning the Egyptians.
6. The Israelite women, led by Miriam (here called "Aaron's sister"), danced and sang to celebrate their safe deliverance from slavery.

(B) Compare two accounts of crossing the Red Sea in Exodus 14 and in Exodus 15.

● What details does each have that the other omits? List these on a board or newsprint as class members call them out.

● Ask class members if they see any apparent contradictions between the two accounts. What are they?

● Ask if any such omissions or contradictions are important enough to raise questions about the significance of the event for Israel.

Dimension 2:
What Does the Bible Mean?

(C) Take a brief look at Bible poetry.

Many of the differences in the two versions of the crossing of the Red Sea can be accounted for by the fact that Exodus 14 is a prose account and Exodus 15 is poetry.

- Ask the class members to list characteristics of English poetry that tend to be found less often in prose, such as
  a. rhyme
  b. meter/rhythm
  c. more figures of speech
  d. "unusual" words
  e. "compressed" syntax

- List these characteristics on board or newsprint.

- In groups of two or three ask class members to pick out figures of speech, unusual word order, and any other poetic characteristics that can be seen in Exodus 15.

- Allow time for groups to report to the whole class.

(D) Contrast prose with poetry.

- Someone may raise the issue of whether a prose account or a poem is "better" or which is "really true."

—Ask class members to close their eyes and think of a particular place and a good time they had there. Ask them to imagine they are in that spot again.
  1. "Look" at it from each direction.
  2. "Hear" the sounds of the place.
  3. What do you smell that you associate with this place?
  4. Would you be there alone? Who might be with you?
—Give members a few moments to remember and mentally experience the time and place.
—Ask them to come back to the present. Working in pairs ask them to take turns describing their experience to the other person, who has not been there with them.

- Find and bring to class several different items that symbolize the sort of spot that you as teacher particularly enjoy, such as the seashore, the solitude of the desert, or the bustle of a city. If you choose the seashore for an example, you might

—put up travel posters of beaches;
—mark a highway map with directions to get there from your location;
—copy the poem "The Sea" by Katherine Mansfield on the board so everyone can read it easily;
—have a tape of Vaughn Williams' "Sea Symphony" playing in the background;
—put sand and some seashells on the window sills;
—put a beach towel on a table with a couple of books about the seashore;

—if you dare, you might even wear scuba gear to class!

- After class members have time to look at and listen to the various items, ask them to choose the one that is the "real" or the "true" description of a day at the beach. The point, of course, is that no one method can convey all aspects of any experience and that we need to use all that are available.

(E) Consider possible reasons for the unusual time sequence in Exodus 15.

Perhaps someone in the class has mentioned some of the items in Exodus 15 that do not seem to "fit" its context. In verses 13 through 17, the poem seems to be talking about things in the future as if they are present or even past events. Discuss why this might be so. Some possibilities may be
  1. it is sung in hope;
  2. it is a prediction of what the LORD will do for Israel;
  3. the entire Song of Moses was composed over many generations, with new verses added to commemorate God's continuing actions on behalf of the people.

Although we cannot know for sure, the third possibility seems the most likely in terms of how the whole song came to be written. It is probable that Miriam's Song, Exodus 15:21, is the oldest of all and that over the generations as Israel's deliverance at the sea was remembered, additional acts of God were added to the song.

- If the class composes a psalm (see "K" below), perhaps you could keep it posted and in other sessions add verses to it to commemorate the group's life together.

(F) Discover actions that show trust in God.

The people were frightened at the sea. Who wouldn't be afraid, especially to see Pharaoh's army approaching? Moses tells them all they need to do is to "keep still."

As the study book puts it, "They are given something to do to show their individual trust in God; they are given something to do as a community to show their unity with one another" (page 33).

- List some things God asks people in the Bible to do to show their trust in God as individuals.

- Then list some things that God asks people in the Bible to do to show their unity with one another.

- In her book *Moses: Man of the Mountain* Zora Neale Hurston has Moses say, "Don't they know, Joshua, that God Himself can't save people who won't try to save themselves?" (University of Illinois Press, 1984; page 201).

- Ask class members, "Is this the same thing as saying 'God helps those who help themselves'?"

Dimension 3:
What Does the Bible Mean to Us?

(G) Consider why reform happens slowly.

In the study book under Dimension 3 reference is made to progress or lack of progress in civil rights in the United States. Schools and churches are mentioned as arenas for the struggle.

● Ask if public education or religion has been most guilty of "two steps forward, one step backwards, and another step sideways." Have class members explain their answers.

● Ask how sports and entertainment compare with schools and churches in the area of civil rights.

(H) Consider the place of proverbs in a culture.

Proverbial sayings are often a shorthand way to express larger meanings. Often the folklore of a culture will even have opposite sayings, such as:
—Absence makes the heart grow fonder.
—Out of sight, out of mind.

● Write on board or newsprint, "There are no atheists in foxholes."
   1. Ask for ideas about what that saying means.
   2. What would the opposite saying be?
   3. Find, or compose, sayings for
      a. Exodus 14:5-6
      b. Exodus 14:11

● Write "Better dead than red" on the board.
   1. Is its opposite "Better red than dead"?
   2. What about "Better the devil you know. . ."?
   3. Do any of these seem to fit the mood of the Israelites as they believe themselves trapped between Pharaoh's army and the sea?

(I) Think about how faith develops.

How does a person's or a community's faith develop? This is an important question especially for persons who have trouble believing in signs and wonders.

● Divide the class members into three groups. Have each group look up and read one of the following verses:
—John 17:20
—Romans 10:17
—1 Thessalonians 2:13

● Ask the groups to discuss faith development in the light of their verse. Some questions to keep in mind are

—When we talk about preaching do we mean only what happens in the Sunday morning sermon?
—What is meant by the Word of God? only what is within the covers of the Bible? every word that is in the Bible?

● Come back together and share discoveries and further questions.

(J) Remember times of gratitude.

● Ask volunteers to mention times of great joy in their life, such as
—graduation
—marriage
—birth of a child
—a job promotion

● Ask how they expressed thanks to God.

● How does the congregation as the people of God express thanks and praise?

(K) Write a psalm.

● Give the class members a brief description of biblical Hebrew poetry. (See "Additional Bible Helps," page 21.)

● Get suggestions from class members as to blessings and events for which they want to praise God.

● Write a psalm of praise as a group effort, with people calling out lines or half lines to be written on board or newsprint where all can see.

● Pray the psalm together at the close of the session.

(L) Add actions to praise.

● Use the psalm written above or another joyous psalm.

● Ask one person to read it aloud.

● Invite class members to clap their hands or snap their fingers or tap their feet as it is read again.

● Invite volunteers to get up and move about in various ways as it is read yet again. Some possibilities:
—stand in place and sway
—take slow, careful steps as you move about the room
—dance

● Imagine that no one in the room is able to talk. How many ways can the class think of, and demonstrate, to express joy and praise without using words?

(M) Consider one or more literary quotations.

● Use the following midrash or the quotation from *Moses: Man of the Mountain* to spark discussion.

- When the Egyptians were dying in the sea, all the ministering angels began to sing joyous praises to God, "but He rebuked them, saying, 'The works of My hands are drowning in the sea, and you would utter song in My presence!'" (quoted in *The Book of Legends: Sefer Ha-Aggadah*, edited by Hayim Nahman Bialik and Yehoshua Hana Ravnitzky; translated by William G. Braude; Schocken Books, 1992; page 73).

- [When the Israelites are between the sea and Pharaoh's army]: "Women screamed in open-mouthed terror and whimpered in fear. Men cursed, cried out and milled about in great whorls. Some tried to run away to the woods to hide, others just stood or squatted on the ground in dumb fear. When they saw Moses come among them they crowded about him. Some clung to him while others screamed at him. He shook them off roughly and kept marching towards the rear.

  "'I always told my husband not to bother with this mess,' one woman sobbed. 'I tried to tell him we was getting along all right under the Egyptians. But he was so hard-headed he had to go and get mixed up in it.'...

  "'Didn't I say all along that this Moses was some fake prophet? That god he made up out of his own head—'

  "'Didn't I always tell you all that them Egyptians was nice people to work for? You couldn't find better boss-men nowhere.'...

  "'Didn't I always say we was better off in slavery than we would be wandering all over the wilderness following after some stray man that nobody don't know nothing about? Tell the truth, didn't I always say that?'

  "'I told you all a long time ago that we had enough gods in Egypt without messing with some fool religion that nobody don't know nothing about but Moses. You all just let him make a fool out of you. I always knowed it was some trick in it. That man is a pure Egyptian and Pharaoh is his brother. He just tolded us off so his brother could butcher us in the wilderness. I told you all so.'

  "'You heard me at the meeting distinctly tell that man to leave us alone and let us serve our Egyptian masters in peace, didn't you? We was getting along fine—plenty to eat and a place to sleep and everything. We wouldn't be in the fix we're in right now if that Moses had of let us alone.'

  "'Who asked him to butt in nohow? Our business didn't concern him, did it? It was our backs they was beating. It isn't none of his and if we was satisfied he ought to be tickled to death. Now Pharaoh is going to kill us all'" (*Moses*, pages 232–34).

—"Translate" the argument of each of these speakers into something you have heard people say about conflict situations.

—"Translate" any that make you recall something you yourself have said on occasion.

(N) Close the session.

- About five minutes before the end of the class period, ask each person to reflect on what has gone on during the hour. Go around the room and ask each person to mention one thing he or she wants to continue to think about or pray about during the coming week.

Additional Bible Helps

Hebrew Poetry

Biblical Hebrew poetry does not rhyme. It has meter or rhythm, but not in the same way as English nursery rhymes or most of our familiar hymns. The major characteristic of Hebrew poetry is called *parallelism*. It is a pattern of making a statement and then matching it with a second statement that usually adds a shade of meaning to the first in the way it is restated. Sometimes instead of two matching lines there will be three.

Suppose we say, for instance,

"It is a sunny day;
   there is not a cloud in the sky."

We have given more information in the second line. The second line adds to what the first line says. That is, it is possible that on "a sunny day" there still could be some clouds. By saying "there is not a cloud in the sky," we sharpen the description of the first line.

For a biblical example, look at the first verse of the Song of the Sea (Exodus 15:1):

"I will sing to the LORD, for he has triumphed
   gloriously;
   horse and rider he has thrown into the sea."

The first line speaks of God's victory; the second gives a detail that makes it specific to this particular instance.

Look now at the second half of verse 2:

"this is my God, and I will praise him,
   my father's God, and I will exalt him."

"My God" in the first line is parallel to "my father's God" in the second line. Do you see how this extends the meaning? In a compact way it conveys the idea that this God is not a new invention or a new discovery but is the same God known by the poet's ancestors in years past.

A second way of relating the lines occurs less often. Sometimes the second line has a similar meaning as in the first case, but it is expressed in the opposite form. The "sunny day" example could have said

"It is a sunny day;
   indeed there is no rain in sight."

This time the second line develops the thought of the first by use of a contrast. What difference does it make? Well, suppose in the first instance that this is the morning of the Sunday school picnic. In that case, either version would work nicely. But what if we were in the middle of a terrific drought? Then the second version, with its mention of the lack of rain, might be more appropriate. Of course "there is not a cloud in the sky" conveys the same information. Remember that poetry has as one intention to impart more than factual information alone.

A biblical example is found in Psalm 1:6.

"for the LORD watches over the way of the righteous,
but the way of the wicked will perish."

Red Sea/Sea of Reeds

Most English translations use the designation "Red Sea" in places such as Exodus 13:18 and 15:22. However, the Hebrew does not say "Red" Sea but rather "Reed" Sea. What are some explanations?

Red and *reed* certainly are close in English. Could that be true in Hebrew also? Alas, no. *Red* would translate "edom" whereas *reed* translates "suph." Even in the Hebrew alphabet, it would be impossible to mistake one for the other.

Since translations as ancient as the Greek Septuagint and the Latin Vulgate say *Red*, doesn't that make them right? No, the argument from age cuts both ways: the Hebrew is the oldest of all.

The Israelites were not a maritime people. They did not make vocabulary distinctions between *sea* and *lake*, for instance. They tended to call any big body of water *sea*, as we tend to lump together several distinct Hebrew words as "locust."

We need also to remember that we have very little idea of the exact spot most ancient place names referred to. Mapmakers put a discrete dot on paper to signify a town, but in many cases it should be more of a generalized smudge. We often know only the general area. Since bodies of water and towns are often referred to with relative descriptions, not knowing the precise location of one hinders the precision of locating the other.

A map of the Sinai peninsula and the northern part of the Red Sea will add some understanding. The body of water we now call the Red Sea is about a hundred miles wide. At the northern end are two inlets, the Gulf of Suez on the west and the Gulf of Aqaba on the east. The mystery of how the crossing of the water occurred is beyond human understanding, but if the Israelites walked on the sea bed of the Red Sea for a hundred miles the time required to move such a large group of people is bewildering. They would have completed that phase of their journey somewhere in Arabia, a long distance from where they were going, with none of the geographical markings of the route we read about in Exodus. Even if they crossed the Gulf of Suez, which might be considered part of the Red Sea, they would have had to travel between fifteen and twenty miles across land that had been covered by ocean a short time before.

Neither the location nor the depth of the water diminishes what God did for the Israelites: they were freed from bondage in Egypt.

5

Exodus 15:22-25; 16:2-3, 11-21, 27-30

NOW WHAT?

LEARNING MENU

Keeping in mind the ways your class members learn best, as well as their needs and interests, choose at least one learning segment from each of the three Dimensions.

Dimension 1:
What Does the Bible Say?

(A) Discuss questions in Dimension 1 of the study book.

- Questions 1 and 2 deal with thirst and with water that looked refreshing but was so bitter "they could not drink." Help the class members go beyond quick, surface answers to the question about Marah. For three days the Israelites had been moving further from the Red Sea. They found no water. Ask each class member to think of a word that might describe his or her feelings at the end of the second day. Then ask for another word from each class member when they reach Marah. What is their reaction before they taste the water at Marah, before they realize it is too bitter to drink? Then God

shows Moses a piece of wood that, when thrown into the water, takes away the brackish taste.

- In Questions 3 and 4 hunger is the complaint. God's answer is to send quails in the evening, manna in the morning.

- Question 5 may be the most surprising: manna is provided morning after morning, but to keep the Israelites mindful of the sabbath, no manna falls on day 7. God provides extra manna on day 6, so Israel will not forget God's special day of rest.

(B) Think about how the miraculous is dealt with in Exodus.

- Divide class members into groups of three or four. Ask them all to turn to Exodus 16:11-21 in their Bibles.

- Tell half the groups to write a headline and an opening paragraph for the manna story as they think the New York *Times* might report it. Tell the other groups to compose a headline and opening paragraph as they would expect it to appear in the *National Enquirer*.

- Come back together and share the results.
—Which style do they think the biblical account itself is closer to?
—What difference does that make?

(C) Think about meanings of *test* and *proof*.

- Write *test* and *proof* on the board or newsprint. Ask class members whether they think of these words as positive or negative.

- Next, ask class members to come up with as many uses of *test* and *proof* as possible, writing their answers on the board or newsprint. Some answers may be
—test pilot
—page proofs
—proofing yeast
—proofs from the photographer
—test kitchen
—mid-term test

- Add proverbs or sayings to the list, such as "The proof is in the pudding" and "The exception that proves the rule."

- Which words and sayings are negative and which are positive in connotation?

- See if the results of this last question match those of the first comparison in this activity. If they do not, ask for opinions about what makes the difference.

(See "Additional Bible Helps," page 26, for more information on the biblical terminology of "testing.")

(D) Examine samples of Jewish lore about manna.

Midrashim are Jewish stories, legends, and wise sayings collected and repeated since the fifth century A.D. Each midrash serves as a commentary on some part of the Hebrew Scriptures. Several of these midrashim, both ancient and of more recent origin, are about manna.

Dailiness of Manna

"The disciples of Rabbi Simeon ben Yohai asked him: Why did the manna not come down for Israel just once a year? He replied: Let me answer you with the parable of a mortal king who had a son. When the king provided him with his sustenance once a year, the son visited his father only once a year. When the father began to provide him with his sustenance daily, the son had to call on his father every day. So it was with Israel. If an Israelite had, say, four or five children, he would worry, saying: Perhaps the manna will not come down tomorrow, and all my children will die of hunger. And so [because the manna was coming down daily] the Israelites were compelled to direct their hearts to their Father in heaven [every day]."

"Still another reason [for daily manna]: To lighten the burdens that had to be carried during the journey."
(From *The Book of Legends, Sefer Ha-Aggadah: Legends from the Talmud and Midrash*; edited by Hayim Nahman Bialik and Yehoshua Hana Ravnitzky; translated by William G. Braude; Schocken Books, 1992; page 75.)

"The Manna Tree"

"This tree, which grows only in the Garden of Eden, supplied food and sustenance to the Israelites in their wanderings. Every evening, at the command of the Holy One, the Manna tree cast forth its fruit into the waiting winds so that the Manna would arrive early the next morning, before the sun rose. Then the Israelites collected it and ate it at once, for if exposed to the sun it melted, like a dream lost between sleeping and waking.

"That is because the fruit which grows on this tree is the most perishable of all fruits, the myriad of images that exist in all the worlds. For the fruit is constantly being transformed on the branches, with all the images of creation taking form. But at the moment the Manna is cast into the wind, it assumes the shape held at the moment it was released.

"A dew preceded the fall of the Manna in the night. This dew was the tears of the Messiah, who exhorted the Holy One to command the Manna tree to set free its fruit. And it was known among the people that so responsive was the Holy One to the tears of the Messiah, that as long as the dew fell, the Manna would soon follow.

"There was no need to cook or bake the Manna, nor did it require any other preparation, and still it contained the flavor of every conceivable dish, and those who tasted of it became equal in strength to the angels. Nor was the Manna wasted when it melted, for out of the melting Manna were formed pools of living water, which also sustained the Children of Israel in their wanderings." (From *Adam's Soul: The Collected Tales of Howard Schwartz*; Jason Aronson, Inc., 1992; page 50.)

> ## "The Gathering of the Manna"
>
> "The gathering of manna caused little trouble, and those among the people who were too lazy to perform even the slightest work, went out while manna fell, so that it fell straight into their hands. The manna lasted until the fourth hour of the day, when it melted; but even the melted manna was not wasted, for out of it formed the rivers, from which the pious will drink in the hereafter." (From *The Legends of the Jews*, by Louis Ginzberg; Volume III; Jewish Publication Society of America, 1942; page 45.)

(E) Discuss the midrashim about manna.

If you or a class member has read aloud one or more of the midrashim about manna (see the sidebars on pages 24–25), discuss with the class members

—What are some of the questions being answered by means of these stories?

—What are some of the differences among the Midrash stories? How is it possible to have manna described in such diverse ways?

—These stories are clearly in the realm of folktales, and so the issue is not which story is "true," making all the others "false." What are some of the uses of such stories?

—Might it be accurate to call some of these stories "parables"?

—Have the class members suggest some other questions about manna that might be asked and answered by means of a folktale.

—Ask class members to compose the outline of a story to answer one of the questions they came up with in response to the previous question.

(F) Roleplay biblical scenes.

● Ask for volunteers to act out Exodus 15:23-25, with individuals taking the parts of Moses and God and the rest of the class "murmuring."

—What does Moses say in verse 25?

—What does God reply?

● Next, move to Exodus 16:2-3.

—Does the murmuring of the crowd become louder? more insistent?

—Do Moses and Aaron say anything to God? (Note that there is no direct speech reported, but that the account skips immediately to God's speech to Moses in verse 4.)

—Is God's response in the same tone of voice as in Exodus 15:24-25? Is God perhaps becoming more impatient?

● Finally, act out Exodus 16:27-29.

—Are the participants speaking in just the same manner as in the two previous episodes?

—If there are differences, what has caused them?

—Do the differences seem to the class to be justified?

Dimension 3: What Does the Bible Mean to Us?

(G) Discuss study book questions.

● See if any class members wish to discuss the questions and issues raised in the study book under Dimension 3.

(H) Clarify understandings of *wilderness*.

● Ask a class member to look up *wilderness* in a Bible dictionary and give the class a brief description of what the wilderness was like.

(Wilderness soon came to be used as a figure of speech to represent the opposite of the Promised Land.)

● In groups of three or four, ask class members to write a brief description of what they might consider to have been a "wilderness" or a "promised land" in their own lives. What does each feel like?

● Make two columns on the board or newsprint, headed "Wilderness" and "Promised Land." Let class members call out descriptions of places and/or events in the world today that would qualify as one or the other.

● Is it possible to be living part of your life in the wilderness and part in the Promised Land all at the same time?

● If the wilderness included signs of God's grace and care, does that mean it is not necessarily bad to be living in the wilderness?

(I) Think about the relevance of manna today.

According to the Bible, the manna lasted only some forty years (Exodus 16:35; Joshua 5:12). It stopped after the people reached the Promised Land and were able to gather their first harvest.

● Ask the class to list characteristics of manna, such as

—provided by God and unexplainable by the people at the time

—necessary to sustain their life

—attended by restrictions by which they could show their faith in God's continuing care.

- Ask for examples of anything since then, either in history, or in their own lives, which might be said to correspond to manna.

- To what extent does the bread in Holy Communion fulfill the same role as manna in the wilderness?

- Manna as "bread from heaven."
—Write "Exodus 16:4" and "Psalm 105:40" on the board.
—If hymnals are available, have the class turn to the hymn, "Guide Me, O Thou Great Jehovah" (No. 127 in *The United Methodist Hymnal*). Use verse 1. (If hymnals are not available, write the verse on the board or newsprint.) Do you think the author, William Williams, had manna in mind when he wrote "bread of heaven"? Might he have had more than manna in mind?
—Ask the class members to look at John 6:31-51. Manna in the wilderness is certainly referred to here. What new interpretation does Jesus put on it?
—In some churches, the words of distribution at Communion are "The Body of Christ, the bread of heaven." Do you think this is meant to refer to manna as well as to Jesus? If it does remind us of manna as well as of Jesus, what additional meanings may Communion have for us?

(J) Think about two rules applying to manna.

- Remind class members of the two "rules" about manna: that on days 1 through 5 they were to gather one day's supply and that on day 6 they should gather enough for two days (Exodus 16:4-5). The study book suggests that these rules are to prevent hoarding, to live in God's daily provision and grace, and to provide a day of rest from daily labor for everyone in the community.

- If the class has discussed activities "H" and "I," ask them now to think of them in terms of the "two manna rules."
—What would "hoarding manna" represent today?
—The study book refers to several passages of Scripture touching on "the increasing gap between rich and poor" (top of page 42). Assign five groups of class members these passages. Ask them to read the passage, discuss its message, and report what the passage seems to say.

    Isaiah 5:8-9
    Jeremiah 17:11
    Amos 5:11-12
    1 Timothy 6:6-10
    2 Corinthians 8:15
—Do any of these verses say anything about who should be able to come to the Lord's Table?

—If sabbath rest is supposed to be for the entire community, even the slaves and the aliens, how can a similar inclusiveness be part of our contemporary manna?

(K) Allow time for reflection and sharing.

- About five minutes before the end of the class period, ask each person to reflect on what has happened during the hour. Ask for volunteers to tell what ideas from today's session they think they will ponder during the coming week.

- Ask everyone to bring in an item to the next class meeting that symbolizes manna in her or his life.

Additional Bible Helps

Testing

Test and *tempt* seem to be used almost interchangeably in English. Partly because *tempt* is nearly always negative, *test* has also come to be seen as negative. If testing is wrong, then surely it is wrong for the people to "test" God.

But what about those cases where God is said to "test" humans? In Exodus 16:4 God announces a test of the people, to see "whether they will follow my instruction or not." In Genesis 22:1, God is said to have tested Abraham, without specifying at the start the nature or purpose of the test. If testing is something people should not do to God, is it fair for God to do it to people?

We must say at the outset, of course, that God has the right to do whatever God wants to do. God does not need to ask our permission first. But since we are encouraged in both testaments to try to be like God, this is not a frivolous question.

Once again, *test* is a word that has more than one meaning. No, it is not a good idea to "test" the LORD by seeing how far we can go in what we know to be a negative direction before provoking God's reaction. But there are times when testing is a good thing because we need to know something that can be disclosed only by a test. To determine if a person is anemic, only a blood test can tell for sure.

Is a new airplane safe? We certainly hope it will be tested strenuously before we ride in it.

Testing is more complicated in personal relationships. A child may test the limits set by the parents and in the process may test the parents' patience! It is well known that children need limits. They also need to push against those limits from time to time. They need to learn that even when they go too far and provoke a negative reaction, the parents still love them. At the same time, they need to learn not to push every limit every time.

Learning needs to be done on both sides of the relationship as the parents also need to know that the children can be trusted.

These ideas are expressed in different ways in the Bible. In Genesis 22 the testing is for the sake of both God and Abraham. God will learn that Abraham is truly devoted; Abraham will learn that God does not require the sacrifice of children.

In Exodus 16 God will learn that some of the people are like young children in the push-against-all-boundaries stage. Some of the people will not follow instructions.

- Maybe they are simply curious: they want to see what will happen if they try to save manna overnight.

- Maybe they do not believe there will be a new supply each day, and so they are taking out "famine insurance."

- Maybe they were not paying attention when Moses explained the rules.

- Maybe they are people who think rules are only for the other guys.

The people also learn things in Exodus 16. They learn that God can be trusted to do as they have been promised. They learn that even their disobedience does not cause the LORD to abandon them. They learn that God knows they need to eat and cares enough for them to make sure they can obtain food.

What about the criticism of the people that they test the LORD too much? There is a point where the second, negative, meaning of the word comes into play. Sometimes people refuse to learn, or refuse to believe what has already been tried and found true.

The first few times the people cry for food or water, they are testing in an all-right sense. They need to know what will happen. But after they have seen God's provisions for them again and again, it is time to be quiet. Then their complaints become negative testing; then they take on the character of "I dare you to continue to be gracious to us, God, when we keep carping at you and Moses."

Enough Is Enough
Within the Scripture there seems to be an ongoing concern that things be shared, that nothing be wasted, and that no one be left out. In terms of food, this can be traced from the regulations about the Passover lamb (Exodus 12:3-4), to the manna accounts in this chapter, to gleaning rules in Leviticus (Chapter 10 of this study), to Jesus' feeding miracles recounted in the Gospels where the leftovers are carefully picked up. In Matthew 14:20, Mark 6:30, and Luke 9:17, the fact of the leftovers being gathered is merely noted. In John 6:12 it is Jesus who says to the disciples, "Gather up the fragments left over, so that nothing may be lost."

6

Exodus 19

BEING CHANNELS OF BLESSING

Dimension 1: What Does the Bible Say?

(A) Compare answers to study book questions.

The answers to the four questions for this session are easy to locate in Exodus 19. God speaks to Moses from the mountain. God's words are to be repeated "to the house of Jacob . . . tell the Israelites." The content of the message repeats the covenant. The people are expected to do two things: obey God's voice and keep the covenant. God will make them "my treasured possession out of all the peoples . . . a priestly kingdom and a holy nation."

God makes clear, lest any assume that God is a regional God who cares about Israel alone, that "indeed, the whole earth is mine." Israel is special, but centuries will go by before the special role is understood as it applies to other nations, to "the whole earth."

Moses gives God's message to "the elders of the people," but the answer comes from all the people, who answered unanimously, "Everything that the LORD has spoken we will do."

(B) Outline Exodus 19:3-8.

● Because the ordering of events in this chapter is so important, write an outline of Exodus 19:3-8 on the board or newsprint with the class members' help, paying careful attention to who says what and when. Important events unfold within these five verses.

(C) Identify the three parts of the covenant.

● List on the board or newsprint the three parts of the covenant with Abraham in Genesis 12:
  1. land (Genesis 12:1b);
  2. descendants (Genesis 12:2a);
  3. to be a blessing to all the families of the earth (Genesis 12:2b, 3b).

Dimension 2:
What Does the Bible Mean?

(D) Review God's actions since Exodus 1.

The LORD begins by telling Moses to have the people recall God's gracious actions on their behalf (Exodus 19:4).

- Ask the class members to make a list of what God has done on Israel's behalf from the beginning of the Book of Exodus.
- Expand the list by going back to the Book of Genesis.

(E) Use the hymnal to review the symbol of "eagle wings" and the concept of "holy nation."

- If hymnals are available and especially if the hymn is familiar to most of your group, sing or read the words to "Holy, Holy, Holy" (No. 64 in *The United Methodist Hymnal*). Does any part of the hymn take on new meaning after studying this chapter? Then turn to the hauntingly beautiful chorus, "On Eagle's Wings" (No. 143, *The United Methodist Hymnal*). If the song is not familiar, ask a soloist to sing it, or listen to a recorded version. Read Exodus 19:3-6 to provide the scriptural setting for the song.

Dimension 3:
What Does the Bible Mean to Us?

(F) Examine class members' symbols of manna.

- As a way of reviewing from last session, ask people to show and describe the things they have brought that symbolize manna for them.

(G) Add to list of God's actions.

- Return to the lists you made in activity "D." Ask class members to expand the list once again by putting on it things God has done for them at any point in their lives.

(H) Review questions from Dimension 3 in study book.

- See if any class members wish to discuss the questions and issues raised in the study book under Dimension 3.

(I) Clarify the sequence of God's actions.

It is vitally important to remember that God freed the Israelites from slavery in Egypt *before* offering them the covenant. Thus, when the covenant did come, it was not like the stereotyped mafia boss saying, "I'm going to make you an offer you can't refuse."

- Ask for two volunteers to take the roles of a parent and a teenager. The parent is offering a special gift to the child.
—The first task is for the class as a whole to decide what the gift should be:
  —a separate telephone line?
  —a car?
  —complete tuition to college?
—The conversation should first take place as "realistically" as the participants can make it. The parent sets the conditions ("No long distance calls; no 900 number calls") and the child tests the limits ("You mean I can't even call Grandma? You know she'd love to hear from me").
—Next ask the volunteers to change the conversation so that the parent's gift is completely without conditions of any kind. The "parent" tries to convince the "child" that there really are not any strings attached.

- Ask for volunteers to take the roles of God and Moses discussing God's offer of a covenant relationship to Israel.
—First have the conversation proceed along "human" lines.
  1. Would God threaten to send the people back to Egypt if they do not accept the covenant?
  2. Would God sound petulant?
  3. Would God whine?
  4. Would God put on a tremendous show of overwhelming power?
—Now, with God in the more familiar role of gracious sovereign, have Moses ask all sorts of "what if" questions, as if he just cannot believe that God really means the offer to be a free offer. For instance: "Come on, God, you can level with me. What will you *really* do if the people say no?"

- Now ask "God" and "Moses" (perhaps new volunteers) to repeat the conversation, but this time see if Moses can continue to refuse.
—If humans are determined *not* to accept God's offer, will it turn out that God's offer was not really free after all? Will God try to coerce the people into accepting? Will God suggest they at least go along with it for a little while? Will God add promises as more "incentive" for the people's agreement?

—If humans say no, will God ever offer the covenant again?

—Whose will can last the longer: humans' in having their own way, or God's in offering the covenant?

• Ask the rest of the class for their reactions to the conversations.

—Which seemed more "real"?

—Which was more in keeping with the biblical understanding of God's nature?

• Ask "God" and "Moses" to describe their feelings and especially any contrasts they may have observed between the two conversations.

(J) Consider the meaning of "special possession" (Exodus 19:5).

• Ask class members to think of what one thing they would most want to save out of their house if it caught on fire. (Assume that all the people and pets have escaped unharmed.) What makes the item special to them?

—Would they ever consider selling it? Even for a fabulous amount of money?

(K) Consider the meaning of "holy" (Exodus 19:6).

• Divide class members into pairs. Let one person in each pair explain to the other person what "holy" means. Encourage each listener to ask questions until the concept is understood.

• Switch roles. But this time, the person who is listening will pretend to be a first-grader. Again, the listener should ask questions until gaining an understanding (on a six-year-old level, that is!).

(L) Consider the meaning of "kingdom of priests" (Exodus 19:6).

• *Priest* is a difficult word for some Protestants to handle.

—What do you call the ordained leader of your congregation?

—If it is something other than *priest*, would you be comfortable changing the title to *priest*?

—Would Exodus 19:6 mean the same thing to you if it said Israel was to be a "kingdom of pastors"? How about a "kingdom of preachers"? a "kingdom of ministers"?

—Find a word or words that best convey to the class members what God is seeking here.

• If priests (or whatever term the class members would rather use) are to be channels of God's grace to the community, then a "kingdom of priests" should spread God's grace to the other nations. Discuss specific ways this might take place, beginning in your own neighborhood.

(M) Recall special preparations to appear before God.

• Ask class members to share any "getting ready for Sunday" rituals they remember from their childhood.

• Are things the same for them now? If not, in what ways have they changed? What do they think has caused the changes?

• Do they think God will accept someone in dirty, ragged clothes as well as someone in Sunday best? If so, would they be willing to come to church next Sunday all ragged and unkempt looking? If not, why not?

• What would probably be the reaction of your congregation to someone who looked poor, dirty, perhaps even homeless?

• If the preparations detailed in Exodus 19:10 are to show respect for God, what are some other ways of showing that respect besides having a special Sunday wardrobe?

(N) Talk about the third part of the covenant.

• Most people familiar with the Bible can name, fairly readily, the first two parts of God's covenant: land and family. The third part, that of being a blessing or being a channel of God's blessing, is much less often remembered. Have the class members test this.

—If your class meets on Sunday morning where there are other adult classes also in session, then with prearranged permission of the various teachers, have pairs of class members visit the other classes for a few minutes. Ask, "What are the three parts of the covenant God made with Abraham, Isaac, and Jacob?"

—When the class reconvenes, let them share their results. Do they find any pattern? Did everyone know the answer quickly?

• Divide the class into groups of three or four. Rewrite the terms of the covenant, changing the wording in order to keep the same understood meaning.

• Again in groups of three or four, put the three parts of Exodus 19:5-6 in terms that would be more easily understood today. Be sure the third part is understood as having the same meaning as Genesis 12:3: "and in you all the families of the earth shall be blessed."

(O) Discuss the Israelites' quick, unanimous promise.

- In Exodus 19:8 the Israelites answered immediately and positively. You may wish to ask the class:
- —Do you think they may have answered hastily? Should they have waited until they knew more of what God was going to ask of them?
- —At what age do children in your faith tradition make their adult profession of faith? (or "are confirmed" or "join the church," depending on the vocabulary of your location?) Why is this the typical age?

  Some churches confirm sixth graders. Do you think this is too soon? Should they wait until they are older and have a better idea of what they are agreeing to?

(P) Consider a midrash interpretation with gender implications.

" 'Thus thou shalt say to the house of Jacob' " (Exod. 19:3)—that is, to the women, meaning that God said to Moses: Tell them those essentials that they can understand; 'and tell the children of Israel' (ibid.), that is, the men, meaning: You may tell them also specific details of precepts, which they [unlike women] can understand. [Midrash separates responsibilities by gender, but Scripture does not.]

"Another explanation: Why did He mention the women first? Because they are prompt in fulfilling commandments.

"Still another explanation: In order that they might lead their children to the study of Torah" (quoted in *The Book of Legends: Sefer Ha-Aggadah: Legends from the Talmud and Midrash*; edited by Hayim Nahman Bialik and Yehoshua Hana Ravnitzky; translated by William G. Braude; Schocken Books, 1992; page 80).

(Q) Identify memorable ideas.

- A few minutes before the end of the class period, ask each person to reflect on what has gone on during the hour. Going around the room, ask them to mention one thing they will continue to think about during the coming week.

(R) Ask class members to bring symbols next time.

- Ask each person to bring in something next week that symbolizes—for him or her at least—one of the three things God is offering to make Israel: either "special possession," "holy," or "a kingdom of priests." Ask them to be ready to tell the class why they have chosen their particular item or items.

Covenant Form and Ancient Vassal Treaties

"Covenant" is an important concept in the Bible. It is possible that the Israelites may have copied some of the form their covenants took from some of the nearby cultures. The content of Israelite covenants, however, is quite different.

Archaeologists have discovered some ancient Akkadian and Hittite vassal treaties that show some similarities to what we find in Exodus. They tend to have five parts:

1. *Preamble*, in which the maker of the treaty is identified. Usually this is an overlord or victorious king.

2. *Historical introduction*, which recounts the history of the relationship between the two parties. It most often extols the virtues of the overlord and reminds the underlings that they are nothing in comparison.

3. *Stipulations* that specify the "rules and regulations" of the continuing relationship. This often includes an amount of tribute money to be paid annually. A major stipulation is that the vassal is not to make a treaty with anyone else without the overlord's permission.

4. *Calling of gods to be witnesses*. The gods of both parties are invoked to keep track of all the vassals. In case the overlord is tricked by anyone, one of his gods is sure to be aware of the treachery and to punish that person severely.

5. *Curses and blessings* are listed for the underlings: curses if they break any of the stipulations and blessings if they follow everything to the letter.

It should be emphasized that these "forms" are not recipes that have to be followed slavishly. There is quite a bit of room for variation. Fairy tales are an example of a form the class will be familiar with. They tend to begin "Once upon a time" and to end "And they lived happily ever after." A story with that beginning and that last line will be recognized as a fairy tale. Still, there is space for infinite variation within that form.

Here are some excerpts from a treaty between the Hittite King Mursilis and Duppi-Tessub of Amurru.

Preamble

"These are the words of the Sun Mursilis, the great king, the king of the Hatti land, the valiant, the favorite of the Storm-god, the son of Suppiluliumas, the great king, the king of the Hatti land, the valiant."

Historical introduction

"Aziras was the grandfather of you, Duppi-Tessub. He rebelled against my father, but submitted again to my father. When the kings of Nuhassi land and the kings of Kinza rebelled against my father, Aziras did not rebel. As he was bound by treaty, he remained bound by treaty. . . .

"When your father died, in accordance with your father's word I did not drop you. . . . To be sure, you were sick and ailing, but although you were ailing, I, the Sun, put you in the place of your father and took your brothers (and) sisters and the Amurru land in oath for you."

Stipulations

"But you, Duppi-Tessub, remain loyal toward the king of the Hatti land, the Hatti land, my sons (and) my grandsons forever! The tribute which was imposed upon your grandfather and your father—they presented 300 shekels of good, refined first-class gold weighed with standard weights—you shall present them likewise. Do not turn your eyes to anyone else! Your fathers presented tribute to Egypt; you [shall not do that!] . . . [With my friend you shall be friend, and with my enemy you shall be enemy.] . . .

"If anyone utters words unfriendly toward the king of the Hatti land before you, Duppi-Tessub, you shall not withhold his name from the king."

Invocation of the gods

There are thirty-six lines of gods and goddesses named in the translation, as well as some breaks in the text. It ends:

"[T]he gods and goddesses of the Hatti land, the gods and goddesses of Amurru land, all the olden gods, Naras, Napsaras, Minki, Tuhusi, Ammunki, Ammizadu, Allalu, Anu, Antu, Apantu, Ellil, Ninlil, the mountains, the rivers, the springs, the great Sea, heaven and earth, the winds (and) the clouds—let these be witnesses to this treaty and to the oath."

Curses and blessings

". . . Should Duppi-Tessub not honor these words of the treaty and the oath, may these gods of the oath destroy Duppi-Tessub together with his person, his wife, his son, his grandson, his house, his land and together with everything that he owns.

"But if Duppi-Tessub honors these words of the treaty and the oath that are inscribed on this tablet, may these gods of the oath protect him together with his person, his wife, his son, his grandson, his house and his country" (from *Ancient Near Eastern Texts Relating to the Old Testament*, edited by James B. Pritchard; Princeton University Press, 1950; pages 203–205).

Continuous Camping

"Camping has become a popular family affair. When vacation time comes many people look forward to pulling a camper or to pitching a tent somewhere for a few days of outdoor living and recreation. Such persons want to have a change of scenery and to get away from their ordinary surroundings and routine activities in order to find a bit of relaxation. The ultimate objective is to recapture freedom. Fresh air and wide open spaces make a strong appeal to those who enjoy camping and to those for whom freedom is meaningful.

"Camping can be fun if everyone works together to share the basic responsibilities. Each one must know what [is to be done], and then each must do his [or her] part. There must also be mutual trust and confidence, and full cooperation, if camping is to be recreational and liberating.

"Contemporary camping, however, is quite different from that which characterized ancient peoples. In antiquity camping was a year-round way of life for nomadic peoples. They chose to live in geographical areas called wildernesses. These were uninhabited areas except when nomads wandered through them in search of food or water. Only temporarily did such wanderers settle down.

"For most people of the twentieth century continuous camping would not be very appealing. Nor would many people today be enticed to camp for any great length of time in a wilderness. Yet, archaeologists, who recover evidences from past civilizations, frequently have to camp in deserted areas which are quite removed from the comforts of civilization. They, perhaps more than other campers, know something of what it must have been like to be continuous campers.

"It is generally agreed that an excellent way to understand how other people live is to try to live as they do. To be deprived of the so-called necessities of life will give one a firsthand sympathy for others who do not have access to such possessions. To participate in the way of life which the wilderness imposes on campers will enable Bible students to understand and to appreciate the wilderness experiences of the ancient Hebrews. Hence, with a camper's outlook, a more sympathetic approach may be made to a study of this portion of the Old Testament record of Israel in the Wilderness of Sinai and in the adjacent wilderness between Egypt and Palestine."

From *Compass Points for Old Testament Study*, by Marc Lovelace. © Abingdon Press, 1972. Used by permission.

7

Exodus 20:1-19

PROMISES TO KEEP

Dimension 1:
What Does the Bible Say?

(A) Discuss the commandments in the light of Dimension 1 questions.

● In Exodus 19:25 Moses "went down to the people and told them." In the next verse, 20:1, "God spoke all these words." Thunder and the sound of the trumpet are what the people hear in 20:18. They plead with Moses, "Do not let God speak to us or we will die."

The people, then, hear God's words through an intermediary, Moses. The commandments are comprehensive. Somewhere in these instructions every area of human life receives guidance from God. Verses 3-11 deal with relationships between the individual and God. Verses 12-17 deal with relationships between human beings as they live in community as God's holy nation.

(B) Count fingers and test memories.

● Using the ten fingers on their hands, ask each class member to see how many commandments he or she can remember. After a few moments of personal searching, give the entire group a chance to call out all ten.

Dimension 2:
What Does the Bible Mean?

(C) Find various ways to count the commandments.

● Compare the different numbering schemes for the Ten Commandments on the chart in the "Additional Bible Helps" section of this leader's guide, page 37. Consider how the "introductory" verse of Exodus 20:2 applies to our reading of the rest of the commandments.

(D) Consider the negatives and positives in the commandments.

● Meanings are sometimes made clearer by putting things the other way round. Where possible, state each negative commandment positively and each positive commandment negatively. That does not mean make an "Anti-Ten Commandments" with items such as "Thou shalt steal!" or "Do not honor your parents!" Rather, specify what is to be avoided in positive commands and what is to be done in negative ones. For instance, "Do not worship other gods" implies "Worship the LORD, the one true God."

(E) Consider the nature of obedience for Jesus.

● Ask class members to look up John 4:11-12, 4:20, and 4:24. Point out that these verses give insights into the Samaritan faith, a break-off from the religion of Judah centuries before the time of Jesus. The woman at the well traces her heritage back to "our ancestor Jacob," before the commandments were given. She wants to argue with Jesus about the proper place to worship God. She believes that he, a Jew, will tell her she is wrong for worshiping, like her ancestors, "on this mountain" (usually identified as Mount Gerizim). She thinks he will say "that the place where people must worship is in Jerusalem." Jesus, however, tells her neither site in itself makes worship appropriate. "God is spirit, and those who worship him must worship in spirit and truth."

Dimension 3:
What Does the Bible Mean to Us?

(F) Review each commandment and its personal application.

● For each commandment ask class members to ponder these questions:

—What sin does this commandment prompt me to confess?

—What amendment of my life am I challenged to make by this commandment?

● This exercise might be done in a number of ways.
  1. Have paper and pencil for each person. Ask them to answer as if he or she is writing to God alone.
  2. Divide the class into pairs. Ask each person to share the answers with the partner to the extent that they are comfortable doing so.
  3. Make a class list of answers on the board, with people calling out whatever they are willing to share with the group.

● Repeat the procedure just completed, only this time, instead of having people answer as individuals, ask them to think of the commandments in terms of the church. What is the church being called to confess and to amend in its collective life?

(G) Search for false gods in our life today.

● In groups of three, consider the good things in life that may have become false gods. The list might include such things as: the economy, science and technology, denominational affiliation, or patriotism.

There is a rabbinic saying, "It is better to have no god than the wrong god." Some would say that most of our false gods are not bad in themselves, but begin by being actually good. Ask the class how they think we can guard against letting the good become bad.

(H) Discuss art and idols.

● In groups of three or four discuss this question: What are idols today?

There have been at various times groups of Christians who have included statues of saints, stained glass windows, even crosses in this category and thus have outlawed them.

Traditional Judaism has interpreted this commandment in such a way that statues or busts of people are not found in synagogues, although there may well be painted portraits or photographs.

Islamic tradition is the strictest in terms of artworks, outlawing recognizable representations not only of people but of plants or animals as well.

● Allow time for groups to report to the whole class.

(I) Discuss profanity and the use of God's name.

● Ask class members who are willing to tell of an incident when they used language they were later ashamed of. Have the class respond as to whether the commandment about God's name was violated.

● Read the following quotation: "Verbal expression of honest anger may be less profane than the proud and spiteful sweetness we sometimes use to cover our hostility, and it may also be healthier for us and for others with whom we live" (from *Ten For Our Time: A New Look at the Ten Commandments*, by Lowell O. Erdahl; C.S.S. Publishing Co., Inc., 1986; page 24).

● Discuss what constitutes a misuse of God's name.

—Praying for a convenient parking space?

—Telling someone "I know what the LORD wants you to do"?

—Threatening children that if they do not behave, God will punish them?

—Threatening adults that if they don't behave, God will send them to hell?

(J) Discuss Jesus and the sabbath.

● Read the sabbath controversy account in Mark 2:23-27.

—Ask for volunteers to play Jesus and an official. Pay special attention to Jesus' tone of voice and manner. Is he dismayed? angry? sad? perplexed? a patient teacher?

(K) Compare Exodus 20:8-11 with Deuteronomy 5:12-15.

● Print these verses side by side where everyone can read them easily. Explore the differences in these verses, especially in any reason given for keeping a particular commandment.

(L) Talk about "blue laws."

"Blue laws" regulate Sunday activities, such as shopping in retail stores. They originated in colonial New England to enforce moral standards and to prohibit some forms of entertainment or recreation on Sundays. One meaning of the word *blue* is "Puritanical; strict."

● Ask if any class members can report incidents from their childhood that touch on sabbath observance.

● Discuss how children today would view such situations.

● Ask two class members to pretend to be a Jew and a Muslim. Give them time to think of an answer to this question: If our government wants to protect the Christian sabbath, should it also protect the Jewish sabbath and times of Muslim worship? (Muslim males pray at the mosque on Friday noon; this service often includes a sermon. The Jewish sabbath begins at sunset on Friday and continues till sunset on Saturday, the seventh day.)

● If Christians who believe in "blue laws" would all refrain from normal commercial activity on Sundays, would there be any need for legislation to close stores?

(M) See how honor differs from love.

● Would the commandment, "Honor your father and your mother" (Exodus 20:12), be different if it said "Love your parents" instead of "Honor"? If so, how? Since some in the class may already know that the biblical concept of *love* has more to do with loyalty than with happy emotions, you might try another paraphrase to ask this question: Would it mean the same thing to say "Be nice to your parents"?

(N) Study the sixth commandment.

● Have one group read John 8:1-11 and another group read Luke 22:47-51.

● Ask each group to consider its story in the light of the sixth commandment (Exodus 20:13).

● After a few minutes of discussion, ask the two groups to share their observations with one another. Display a sign that says, "Why do people kill people who kill people to show that it's wrong to kill people?" Are there other issues your group may want to address in terms of their coming, or not coming, under the authority of this commandment? What might be said about war? abortion? capital punishment? assisted suicide?

(O) Discuss whether adultery is the only sexual sin needing control by a commandment.

● In small groups, compare this commandment (Exodus 20:14) with Matthew 5:27 and "lustful looking."

● Consider if the commandment has anything to say to current topics of increasing concern, such as sexual harassment, pornography, and clergy sexual misconduct.

● Read the following statement aloud: "Adultery can be committed only by someone who is married." Point out that *fornication* means sexual relations outside of marriage. It is not mentioned in the commandments. Ask if that means adultery is the only sexual sin that *really* matters.

(P) Rate the commandments.

● List the Ten Commandments on the board or newsprint.

● Either in small groups or as a whole class discuss:

—If you were forced to eliminate one commandment, which would it be? Why?

—Continue by elimination until you have built a "relative importance" scale for the commandments.

● If this was done in groups, have the groups share, and defend, their various listings.

● Another way to get to the essence of this activity would be to pretend that one commandment is to be taught each month to all the people in your city. Pretend also that as soon as a commandment is taught, it will be thoroughly and completely obeyed. Decide in which order to teach them.

(Q) Read quotations to spark discussion.

● Divide the class into two, three, or six groups. Give each group one or more of the following quotations from *The Ten Commandments and Human Rights*, by

Dr. Walter Harrelson (Fortress Press, 1980). Ask each group to function as a "jury" and report whether they agree or disagree with their quotation:

1. "Thousands and thousands struggle for health in mental institutions trying to undo, with professional help, the damage done by those who have driven them into psychosis by the warnings of eternal damnation. Unloved in this world by family and friends, as they believe, they have concluded that God too will not love them, cannot love them, until they do what the religious practitioner demands they do. God, too, may then be identified as a deceiver and destroyer. These more subtle ways of abusing the power of God are far more destructive, I believe, than those prevalent in ancient societies" (page 76).

2. "A community that recognizes that one day out of seven belongs to God and that the way to give it to God is to stop doing what one ordinarily does—break with the grasping for food and shelter and a better life, break with all efforts to secure one's place in the world, break with even the normal acts of cult and pilgrimage—such a community knows that life consists of more than work, more than food, more than shelter, more than protection from one's enemies, more than religious rites and sacrifice and prayer. . . . In addition to the need to understand leisure and to do so in relation to the commandment not to work on the seventh day, people today need to discover how to find joy in the work that they actually do. That too depends on a right understanding of the fourth commandment" (pages 84, 87).

3. "And if there is real health in the relation of adult parents to their elderly parents, there will be health in the other relations of the family. For it is how one deals with the helpless, with those who can no longer fend for themselves, and with such helpless ones against whom one has a lifetime of grievances for wrongs done or imagined, that provides the test of one's moral and human commitments. Just as the treatment of orphans, widows, and the poor is the general test of justice within the society, so the treatment of elderly parents by their children is the test of family relations as such" (page 103).

4. "The prohibition against adultery stakes out the claim of the two partners in marriage to a relationship between themselves that is not to be compromised or destroyed by the action of either partner. While the law does allow for the man to marry more than one wife, it specifies limits to his favoring the one over the other" (page 125).

5. "It is self-indulgent and supercilious to speak the truth, no matter what harm ensues, merely to protect one's reputation for veracity" (page 146).

6. "If the hunger for a life like that believed to exist in, say, the United States or Canada or West Germany should overwhelm and threaten to destroy a person from an African or Latin American land, then the commandment not to covet would come into play. But it would be entirely erroneous for the prohibition to be *used* by those who *have* an abundance of the goods of the earth to ward off the legitimate desires of the poor for a fairer share of those goods" (page 152).

Additional Bible Helps

What About Other Gods?

The first commandment makes no argument for or against the existence of other gods. What it commands is the exclusive loyalty and worship of Israel for the Lord regardless of whether other gods really exist. The fancy word for this is "henotheism," which means the exclusive worship of one god regardless of the possible existence of other gods. This makes it different from "monotheism," which maintains that there is only one God. We might ask if the first commandment would be stronger if it also said that there is only one God.

The Ten Commandments—A Treaty?

Using the five-part treaty outline in the "Additional Bible Helps" section of Chapter 6, consider how Exodus 20 may be arranged into those same parts. Do not expect there to be a perfect match, any more than every fairy tale or every piano sonata exactly resembles every other one. There are enough similarities, though, that many people believe the Israelites took a form from the political realm and gave it new theological meaning.

1. Preamble
Exodus 20:2a
2. Historical introduction
Exodus 20:2b
3. Stipulations
Exodus 20:3-17
4. Witnesses
Exodus 20:18

(This portion is not as clear as some of the others. Obviously there cannot be a list of gods to witness the agreement. But there are notices of unusual happenings in the natural world and all the people, not just Moses and other leaders, hear the Lord.)

5. Blessings and curses

(This section is not found within Exodus 20, although there are parts of some commandments that could be included—verses 5 and 12, for example. But there are lists of blessings and curses found elsewhere [Deuteronomy 27:15–28:46, for instance], so that their omission from this particular chapter is not seen to be an insurmountable handicap.)

Numbering the Ten Commandments

The division and numbering of the Ten Commandments by various faith communities is different, although they all come out to the familiar number ten.

Commandment	Contemporary Judaism	Modern Greek and Reformed	Lutheran and Roman Catholic
[Remember] I am the LORD your God who brought you out of the land of Egypt, out of the house of slavery.	1st		1st
You shall have no gods except me.	2nd	1st	1st
You shall not make a carved image . . . or bow down to them . . . or serve them. ∴ . .	2nd	2nd	1st
You shall not misuse the name of the LORD your God.	3rd	3rd	2nd
Remember the sabbath day, and keep it holy.	4th	4th	3rd
Honor your father and your mother.	5th	5th	4th
Do not kill.	6th	6th	5th
Do not commit adultery.	7th	7th	6th
Do not steal.	8th	8th	7th
Do not answer as a false witness against your neighbor.	9th	9th	8th
Do not covet your neighbor's house or wife or anything that is your neighbor's.	10th	10th	9th & 10th

(The Exodus version of commandment 10 places "house" before "wife" in listing things not to covet; in Deuteronomy 5 the order is reversed. Some Christians count "Neither shall you covet your neighbor's wife" as number 9 and other coveting as number 10.)

8

Exodus 31:18–32:14

...AND IF THEY'RE BROKEN?

LEARNING MENU

Keeping in mind the ways your class members learn best, as well as their needs and interests, choose at least one learning segment from each of the three Dimensions.

Dimension 1:
What Does the Bible Say?

(A) Discuss the Dimension 1 questions in the study book.

1. The people were upset that Moses was delayed in coming down from the mountain. They asked Aaron to "make gods for us," for "we do not know what has become of" Moses.
2. Aaron collected all the gold jewelry from the people, formed it in a mold, and "cast an image of a calf." He announced that this was now their god.
3. God was so angry with the people that he planned to destroy them all and start anew with only Moses.
4. Moses begged God to relent, to not destroy the people. He suggested that if God kills the people, the Egyptians

would hear of it and question what kind of god this is. Moses also reminded God of the covenant God had made with Abraham, Isaac, and Israel. "And the LORD changed his mind about the disaster that he planned to bring on his people."
5. When Moses got close to the Israelites' camp, he heard a strange sound, the sound of revelers. When he realized that they were worshiping the calf, Moses smashed on the ground the tablets containing God's words, burned the golden calf, ground it to powder, mixed it in the water, and made the people drink it.

(B) Consider meaning of "the finger of God."

- Ask class members to read in unison Exodus 31:18. Discuss anything that the finger of God suggests to class members. (Something like a laser beam coming from it to carve words into stone? Michelangelo's painting of the creation of Adam? the color of the skin on God's finger?)

- You may wish to point out two other biblical uses of the expression. In Exodus 8:19 Pharaoh's magicians use it to explain their inability to create gnats. In Luke 11:20 we find Jesus asking if people think he casts out demons by the ruler of the demons or by the finger of God.

Dimension 2:
What Does the Bible Mean?

(C) Paraphrase Exodus 32:1-6.

- Before class, prepare a paraphrase of Exodus 32:1-6 using the wordings discussed in Dimension 2 of the study book. That is, it would begin on the order of "the people mobbed against Aaron, . . . And Aaron said to them, 'Tear off the rings of gold. . . .'" Use the options that seem to go easier on Aaron, on making him bear less responsibility for what happens.

- Ask a volunteer to read the verses from the New Revised Standard Version of the Bible.

- Then read your paraphrased version to the class.

- Ask for observations.

(D) Hold a trial for Aaron.

- Divide the class into four groups:
—prosecuting team
—defending team
—witness team
—jury

- Using not only Exodus 32 but any other biblical material the class members want to bring in, give each team about ten minutes to prepare their part of the trial.

- Instead of having an individual play Aaron, let the prosecuting and defending team debate each other, cite evidence, and raise questions. The witness team may be questioned by either side at any time.

- When the jury renders its verdict, ask them to give reasons and not just their decision.

(E) Have a dialogue between God and Moses.

- Ask for two volunteers to act out the conversation between God and Moses on Mount Sinai as recorded in Exodus 32:7-13.

- The first time, ask them to read it sounding as if God really can hardly wait to wipe out Israel and start all over again with Moses.

- A second time let them read as if God really does not intend to destroy Israel but considers this a testing of Moses, somewhat as Abraham was tested in Genesis 22.

- A third time, perhaps with new volunteers, have Moses teeter on the edge of accepting God's offer to wipe out Israel and start again with Moses.

—What causes him almost to accept?
—What causes him to remain loyal to the people in the end?
—When he gets down off the mountain and sees the golden calf, does he ask God to reconsider the offer and wipe the others out after all?

(F) Notice changes in Moses.

- What makes Moses switch from defending the people to God (verses 11-13) to becoming enraged at the people (verses 19-20)? Can the change be justified?

Dimension 3:
What Does the Bible Mean to Us?

(G) Discuss questions and issues from study book.

- Discuss the questions and issues raised in Dimension 3 of the study book.

(H) Carefully examine Exodus 32:5.

- What is Aaron doing here in calling a festival to the LORD?
—Does he think the calf is the LORD?
—Is he now frightened by what is happening and trying to get the people back on the right track by worshiping the LORD instead of the calf?
—Does he know that the calf and the LORD are different but halfheartedly hold to a sort of "the more the merrier" attitude?

- Can we learn anything from Aaron? Perhaps
—how quickly situations can get out of hand
—how hard it is to make sure everyone has the same interpretation of events.

(I) Present Exodus 32:21-24 as a dialogue reading.

- Ask for volunteers to read the conversation between Moses and Aaron.
—Does Moses believe Aaron's story that the golden calf jumped out of the fire all by itself?
—Does Aaron believe the story himself?

- Analyze Aaron's argument. Where in the Bible have you heard the same story before?
—It's the fault of the people; they're basically no good.
—It's Moses' fault for being away so long and not letting any of us know when he was going to get back.

—I threw the gold into the fire to remove temptation from anyone who might have an idea to make an idol, and the calf leaped out all by itself.

- Put the gist of Aaron's three arguments in more contemporary terms.

- Do you see any place in the world today where these arguments are being offered?

—People are no good.

—It's someone else's fault.

—It's no one's fault; it just happened.

(J) Evaluate a difficult portion of Exodus.

Exodus 32:25-29 is a terrible story. Partly because it is so difficult, it is skipped over in the study book. In the limited space of thirteen chapters we certainly cannot cover every episode. This is one, however, that someone may bring up. (If no one in the class does, perhaps the leader should consider whether to deal with it in class time.)

- List on the board or newsprint any possible reasons Moses was justified in instigating this slaughter.

- List any reasons he should not have done it.

- List the unanswered questions class members have about the passage. Where might they go for further assistance?

This is the sort of story that sometimes raises issues of the appropriateness of the Old Testament for Christians. Several positions have been taken throughout history, ranging from belief that the "First Testament" is utterly irrelevant to the Christian to holding that it is absolutely necessary for understanding not only Jesus Christ, but also what God wants from us in all our relationships. Examples of the variety of positions include:

—With Jesus as their Savior, Christians no longer need the Old Testament. Perhaps it can be used to learn some history, but it is mostly full of things that have been superseded with the Incarnation.

—Just because we do not understand something or don't like something does not mean it cannot be a way for God to communicate truth to us. The passages we do not know what to do with now we should pray over and ponder all the harder. After a season it is all right to put them aside, but we dare not throw out any of the Bible.

Read John 16:12-15. There seem to be at least two messages here:

—Even the disciples themselves did not understand everything at once, not even while they had Jesus in person as their teacher.

—We may well be surprised by new teachings, even by those that come through the agency of the Holy Spirit.

—In addition, there may be a time when we do not understand the meaning of a passage. That is all right. Jesus' words in John help our discomfort both with new and strange-sounding ideas from others and with those scripture texts we cannot yet understand ourselves.

(K) Consider Exodus 32:6 and the sequence of events involving the Israelites.

- You will need to have on hand several translations of the Bible. Ask different persons to read this verse from the various Bible translations. What did the Israelites do after they worshiped, ate, and drank? They got up to do what?

- List on board or newsprint the several words that are used to say what the Israelites did.

A strictly literal translation says they "played."

—Can "play" be good? What makes it so?

—Can "play" be bad? Under what circumstances?

—Does it change the meaning of the story to keep the neutral term? to substitute something more specific, especially something with an overtone of illicit sex?

- Ask class members if anyone can see a connection between this episode and the parable of the prodigal son (Luke 15:11-32). Specifically, what did the younger boy do with his money?

—According to his brother (Luke 15:30) he "devoured your property with prostitutes."

—According to Jesus (verse 13) he "squandered his property in dissolute living."

—Someone may be using a Bible that refers to prostitutes or harlots in verse 13. This is a case of a translator's adding the term there since it is used in verse 30. The way Jesus tells the story, the matter is left ambiguous. "Loose living" certainly could involve prostitutes but it doesn't necessarily. In verse 30 the older brother is jumping to that conclusion without evidence. It is a pity when translators unintentionally jump to the same conclusion. Then unsuspecting readers have no way of seeing this gentle point Jesus is making through the accusation of the older brother.

- Ask if anyone would be willing to share an incident of jumping to the wrong conclusion, or taking evidence farther than it would really go. (My younger daughter does this quite often. She hears the back door open and close and starts a scene in the belief that her older sister has gone somewhere without her. Sometimes that may have happened. Usually, however, the sound of the door signals nothing more traumatic than Mom taking something out to the compost pile.)

There is a tradition that after speaking with God on the mountain top, Moses grew horns. This, however, is a misinterpretation of the statement that Moses' face shone (glowed, sent forth beams). The Hebrew words are very similar. (Alinari/Art Resource, NY)

(L) Look at references to the golden calf in literature.

Here are two examples of where the golden calf episode has been used in fiction:

- In Charles Dickens's *Martin Chuzzlewit* the character Mr. Pecksniff says, "The profit of dissimulation! To worship the golden calf of Baal, for eighteen shillings a week!" (Chapter 10).

- In the O. Henry story "The Enchanted Profile," an affluent character is said to be "mighty popular down in the part of town where they worship the golden calf."

—What do you make of the fact that the golden calf seems in these situations to represent wealth?

—Is it the material the calf is made of that leads to this conclusion? That is, would a stone calf or a wooden calf represent quite different things?

- Divide class members into small groups of three to four persons. Ask them to decide what Aaron would be urged to make were he in your community.

—Why do people want an image? ("Moses has been gone so long.")

—What do they want it for? ("We want a god to go before us.")

—What shape should it be in?

—What should it be made of?

—What would its rites and festivities look like?

- After groups discuss the previous questions, ask them to look for answers to this question: Are there any things already in existence that serve the same function in this culture as the calf did in Exodus 32? (Encourage answers that apply to the nation as a whole, to Christianity or its subdivisions, or to individual Christians.)

- If God were to threaten to destroy persons for worshiping whatever the groups identify above, with whom do you think God would start over to make a faithful community?

(M) Close the session.

- In the final few minutes have the class reflect on what has gone on. Ask for volunteers to share which part they think will stick with them through the coming week.

Additional Bible Helps

Who Was the Golden Calf Meant to Be?

There have been a number of suggestions made as to the identity the calf was supposed to symbolize and its intended function.

1. Perhaps the people were intending it to be a substitute, even just a temporary stand-in, for Moses. He had indeed been gone for a long time. ("Forty days and forty nights" [Exodus 24:18] is a proverbial expression for a very long time, similar to the way "a couple of cookies" can refer to three as well as to two.)

The descriptions of Moses in Exodus 32:1 and of the calf in 32:4 are strikingly similar: "who brought you up out of the land of Egypt." Most striking of all is that this phrase is used nearly always in association with the LORD rather than with a person. Indeed, these words are part of God's own primary identity in relationship to the Israelites, serving as a preamble to the Ten Commandments in Exodus 20:2 for example.

The calf that Aaron made was probably a bull calf. A bull is a horned animal, and there is a tradition that after speaking with God on the mountaintop, Moses grew horns (Exodus 34:29-30). This, however, is a misinterpretation of the statement that Moses' face shone (glowed, sent forth beams). The Hebrew words for *horn* and *shone* are very similar.

2. The bull perhaps was a representation of the LORD. Bulls are strong and mighty animals. The LORD is described as mighty in a number of places. See, for instance, Genesis 49:24; Psalm 132:2, 5; Isaiah 1:24; 49:26; 60:16.

The Hebrew words for *bull* and *mighty one* sound similar and come from the same root.

3. Maybe the people meant the bull not to stand for the LORD but to be a seat or a footstool for God. The cherubim on the top of the ark of the covenant, for instance, are said to be God's "footstool" or a meeting place between the LORD and the people (Exodus 25:18-22)

4. Or, as another option, maybe the people thought they were making the animal for God to ride on, as the gods of surrounding cultures were sometimes pictured riding animals that either actually exist or that are imaginary creations. (In 2 Samuel 22:11, the LORD is depicted as riding on a cherub.)

5. All of these suggestions are attractive in that they help get the people off the hook. It is painful to think that so soon after giving their wholehearted assent to the covenant, they would be making other gods. Yet the final possibility, indeed a probability, is that the people really did mean this calf to be or to represent another god. In the neighboring Canaanite gathering of gods both 'El and Ba'al were associated with bulls. 'El is even called "the Bull."

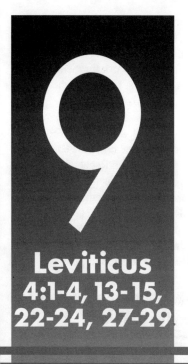

MORE THAN STERILE LEGALISM

Leviticus 4:1-4, 13-15, 22-24, 27-29

Dimension 1:
What Does the Bible Say?

(A) Discuss answers to the questions in the Dimension 1 section of the study book.

1. "What is left" of the offering "shall be for Aaron and his sons," the priests who get their living from the people's offerings, not from land they cultivate nor from livestock they raise.
2. Leviticus 4 notes specifically that if an "anointed priest," "the whole congregation," "a ruler," or "anyone of the ordinary people" sins each must make a sin offering to God.
3. The type of sin offering required depends on what the sinner can financially afford.
4. A thief who is repentant must return what was stolen to the owner plus one-fifth. Then the thief must bring a guilt offering to the priest.

(B) Pantomime Leviticus 1:14-17.

- Ask a member of your class with a flair for the dramatic to read the instruction to the priest for the sacrifice of a turtledove or pigeon in Leviticus 1:14-17.

- Ask that person, by practicing before class time, to be ready to act out in silence (pantomime) the movements of the priest.

- Then call upon the class to suggest what the pantomimist might be doing.

- Read the verses to the class or have them read them in unison.

- If there are questions, record them on the board or on newsprint and promise to discuss them later. (Be sure to schedule time for this discussion so that class members' questions are answered.)

Dimension 2:
What Does the Bible Mean?

(C) Decide on the categories of sin: accidental/intentional; omission/commission.

- Before class begins, write the following on the board or newsprint:
  a. The wedding rehearsal is on Friday.
  b. $1 + 1 = 2$
  c. $1 + 1 = 10$
  d. Enrico left the scene of the accident.
  e. Maggie is pregnant.
  f. Today is Saturday.
  g. Mr. and Mrs. Liu do not pay social security taxes for any domestic employees.
  h. I saw Robert hitting Rachel, but I did not tell anyone.

- Ask the class members to say which items are sins, which are not, and for which ones they need more information. If the latter is the case, you can supply the following additional information:
  a. I got mixed up. The wedding rehearsal is actually on Thursday, not Friday.
  c. The equation is written with "base 2" numbers.
  d. The police officer in charge told Enrico that he was free to go.
  e. Maggie and her husband Tamil have been praying for a child for two years.
  f. This lesson is being written on a Saturday.
  g. Mr. and Mrs. Liu live in Costa Rica.
  h. Robert and Rachel are both two years old.

- After they have discussed the items, change the information on some of them as follows:
  a. The wedding rehearsal is really on Thursday, but I hoped that if I told people it was Friday, then Beth wouldn't show up. She is a gossip and not in the wedding, and I just do not want to have her around.
  d. Enrico does not have a driver's license or automobile insurance. Then add: Enrico was not involved in the accident. OR Enrico was in the accident, but he was riding a bicycle.
  e. Maggie and Tamil are not married, but they love each other very much and live together as husband and wife. OR Maggie and Tamil are married, but the doctor has warned Maggie that another pregnancy would seriously endanger her health. OR Maggie and Tamil are married and healthy, and they have six children already.
  g. Mr. and Mrs. Liu live in the United States and want to pay social security taxes for their employees, but the women who work for them have asked to be paid

"under the table"—in cash, so that they do not have to report their incomes to the government. OR Mr. and Mrs. Liu did not realize that the social security taxes had to be paid for people who work for them only occasionally. OR Mr. and Mrs. Liu live in the United States and have no hired help of any kind.
  h. Robert and Rachel are adults. Then add: Robert and Rachel are adults, and Rachel will not say who beat her up so badly that she is in the hospital. Then add: Robert and Rachel are adults, and Rachel will not say who beat her up so badly that she is in the hospital and Fred has been arrested for it. (Remember the first statement is "I saw Robert hit Rachel.")

- For each item that the class decides is a sin, ask them which of the Ten Commandments it comes under.
- Which of these sins would be covered in Leviticus 1–7?

(D) Apply the Ten Commandments to the previous discussion.

- Do all things that are classified as sins have to come under the jurisdiction of one of the Ten Commandments? (You may want to review some of the discussion in Chapter 7 of this study.)

Dimension 3:
What Does the Bible Mean to Us?

(E) Examine confession and atonement.

- If your church has a "prayer of confession" in the regular Sunday morning worship service, have copies available for everyone. (If the prayer is different each week, use a recent example.)
—How do class members connect the prayer of confession with their own lives?
—Is the prayer so general that it is easy to say without feeling any "pinch"?
—Is it so specific that it is difficult for some people to say out loud?
—Is it so specific about sins that are not their sins that it seems meaningless for some to say?

- In groups of three or four ask class members to compose prayers of confession that would be suitable for the main Sunday service for your entire congregation, being sensitive to the following points:
—Try to make the prayers specific enough that they say something meaningful.
—Try not to make them so specific as to draw attention to particular, easily identifiable, individuals in the congregation.

—Try not to make the prayers so specific as to leave out major portions of the congregation entirely.

(F) Show a concern that no one be left out.

Again and again we see this Old Testament concern that we find ways for every member of the community to take part in everything.

- Divide the class into pairs or into groups of three. Make "name tags" with some of the following designations and give one or more to each group.

    old
    hard of hearing
    crippled by arthritis
    parent of three preschool children
    unemployed
    working two jobs
    working the night shift
    clinically depressed
    blind
    painfully shy
    unable to read
    use a wheelchair

- Have each team note difficulties they might face if they, as persons described above, participated in this class. What might be done to overcome those difficulties?

- If there are class members who fit into any of these categories, ask them for their reactions.

—Does their "label" restrict them more than their reality? That is, do people assume if they see a hearing aid, for example, that the person can hear only if shouted at?

—Are there things that would make their participation in the class easier? more fulfilling?

- Pass out copies of the main worship bulletin or service sheet to the groups. Ask them to see if their "label" conditions would have any effect on their ability to participate fully in worship.

- Depending on the composition of your group and the trust level that has developed, you might want to add other categories relevant to your situation. These are only a few possibilities:

    African American
    Asian American
    Euro-American
    Native American
    Hispanic
    adopted
    single parent
    recovering addict
    abused spouse

(G) Compare Leviticus 6:4-7 and Matthew 5:23-24.

Leviticus 6:4-7 sets the restitution of stolen property to the neighbor before the ritual in the temple.

- Ask the class, What would be an appropriate way to achieve such restitution before going to worship today?

- Read Matthew 5:23-24. What relationship do you think there is between this admonition of Jesus to be reconciled with one against whom you have sinned before offering your gift to God and Leviticus 6:4-7?

(H) Return to the list in "C" of sins and not-sins.

- In groups of three or four, ask the class members to discuss the following questions:
—For each sin, who is the sinner and who is the sinned-against?
—How might the sinner make restitution?
—What is the Christian to do if restitution is impossible?
    a. If the offended person has died?
    b. If the offended person is unwilling to accept the apology or whatever else is offered?
    c. If the offended person is not willing to talk about it at all?

(I) In a time for personal confession, ask class members to identify a sin.

- Make sure each individual has paper and pencil.

- Ask each person to think of some sin he or she committed recently against an individual. It can be as simple as a snappish word spoken to a family member that morning.

- Ask individuals to write on the paper one sentence they would like to say to the person they hurt.

- In a period of silent prayer, suggest they ask God to show them a way to make amends to the offended person.

- Ask them to fold their paper and put it in their pocket or purse. Ask them to carry it with them until they have been able to resolve the matter, continuing to ask God to make an opening for them to repent, apologize, make amends, or whatever matches the individual situation.

(J) Find out what forgiveness of sins means.

- Read the following statement to the class: "Since Jesus' death on the cross was an expiation for the sins of the whole world, what I am required to do is ask Jesus once to forgive me and to be my Savior. Anything more than that—restitution, even confession—is not necessary and even shows I do not really trust Jesus."

- Divide the class into two groups. Let one group study the statement above from the point of view that it is true and complete and the other group from the point of view that it is inadequate.

- After a few minutes in the groups, have the class come together again. Make two columns on the board: "complete" and "inadequate."

—Which parts of the statement do all the class members agree with?

—Which parts do they think are incorrect?

—If incorrect, what makes them so?

    a. They do not go far enough.

    b. They go too far.

    c. They are too open to potentially dangerous misunderstanding.

(K) Look at the practice of confession.

Confession to an individual is part of the practice in many Christian denominations. It can be seen as something of an intermediate point between apology and restitution to the injured party and asking for God's forgiveness.

- See whether any class members were formerly Roman Catholic, Orthodox, or part of any other Christian group that offers or requires some sort of individual confession. If so, ask if they would be willing to share some of their experiences with the rite.

- Ask the pastor to visit the class and discuss your denomination's view of confession.

- Ask a priest from a nearby Roman Catholic, Orthodox, or Episcopal church to discuss other views of confession. (They are not all the same!)

Additional Bible Helps

The Meaning of "Salt" and the "Covenant of Salt"

The study book suggests that the use of salt imagery in different sections of the Bible is related. It further suggests that when God mentions "the covenant" we are supposed to think all the way back to the covenant first made with Abram in Genesis 12 and 17. Finally, it ties these together with Jesus' statement to the disciples in Matthew 5:13: "You are the salt of the earth" and concludes that possibly what Jesus is saying to his disciples and to all future disciples is something like this: "You are supposed to be the sign of God's covenant with the entire world and all the people on earth. You are supposed to be a channel of God's blessing to absolutely everyone on earth."

Bible Interpretation

Is your class struggling with differences of opinion regarding a Christian's freedom to approach biblical interpretation openly and creatively? You may wish to use the article beginning on page 70 of this book. "The Bible Is . . . ," by Dee Baker, gives six perspectives on Bible interpretation sincerely held by Christians who differ with one another. You may wish to make copies of the article and have class members rate themselves, then discuss the reasons we differ.

Interpreting the Bible:
The Writer's Personal Stance

Since neither Leviticus 2:13 or Matthew 5:13 is commonly interpreted as I have done, this may be an appropriate place to say something about my own beliefs when I study a text.

1. It is possible for there to be more than one right answer. Our task when we study the Bible is not to find The-One-and-Only-Right-Answer and then call everyone else's ideas wrong. Our task, rather, is to try to hear what God is saying to us today.

> Prayer for Illumination
> Lord, open our hearts and minds
> by the power of your Holy Spirit,
> that, as the Scriptures are read
> and your Word proclaimed,
> we may hear with joy what you say to us today.
> Amen.

(From *The United Methodist Hymnal;* Copyright © 1989 by The United Methodist Publishing House; page 6.)

2. But having the possibility of more than one right answer does not mean—at least does not mean to me—that all answers are equally good. Some answers I believe are entirely wrong, even if they are deeply cherished by some very good individuals. For example, Great Aunt Hilda may be convinced that the moon is made of green cheese because the Twenty-third Psalm speaks of green pastures. I am not belittling Great Aunt Hilda's love of Jesus or her faithfulness as a Christian when I say I think it's wrong to interpret Psalm 23 as having anything to do with the moon or with cheese.

3. So, if more than one answer can be right, but some can be wrong, how is one supposed to know right from wrong? Certainly the fact that something is printed in a book does not make it automatically correct! Here is how I try to distinguish between right and wrong interpretations.

—I believe that God is faithful. I believe that God does not break promises or take back covenants. Therefore, any interpretation that requires a belief in a broken promise or lie on God's part, I do not believe can be correct.

—I believe that God is not limited by the size of my understanding, nor even by all the interpretations in the whole world. God is able to do something new in interpretation, even something surprising.

—I believe that God calls each of us by name and knows each of us intimately. Therefore, I do not believe that God has a "one size fits all" interpretation of each passage of Scripture. What I need to hear today may be different from what you need to hear today, as indeed it may be quite different from what I myself will need to hear tomorrow. Thus, I need always to be open to new interpretations.

Forgiveness and the Shedding of Blood

Some persons are attracted to Hebrews 9:22, which says: "Indeed, under the law almost everything is purified with blood and without the shedding of blood there is no forgiveness of sins." To me the word *almost* is significant.

Here is how I reason out that position. I always begin by asking the Holy Spirit for guidance in my studies.

I believe the Spirit led me to consider that Leviticus 5:11 says that people who cannot afford animals may make a sacrifice of flour.

There is nothing said about how they are only half-forgiven. Nor are they told to come back later with an animal when they can afford one. Therefore, God must be able to forgive them without the shedding of blood.

Ah, but what about Genesis 3:21 where the LORD God made garments of skins for Adam and Eve when they were expelled from Eden because of their sin. Doesn't this show that from the very beginning sin has to be atoned for by blood? Didn't those skins come from the slaughter of living animals?

I remember that there in the space of three chapters we have had the whole universe created by God's speaking, humans created from river mud and from bone, and even a talking serpent. Is it too hard to believe that a God who could do all that could find a way to make fur coats without killing animals to get the fur?

Please understand that I am not saying that the Crucifixion is without value; I am not denying the power of Jesus' shed blood. What I am trying to say is that we need to be careful lest we try to trap God in the boxes of our own beliefs. That will only trap us and bind us in the end.

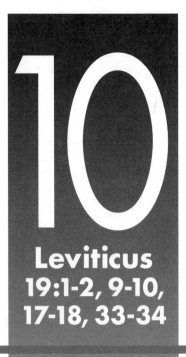

10

Leviticus
19:1-2, 9-10,
17-18, 33-34

NEIGHBORS AND STRANGERS

LEARNING MENU
Keeping in mind the ways your class members learn best, as well as their needs and interests, choose at least one learning segment from each of the three Dimensions.

Dimension 1:
What Does the Bible Say?

(A) Discuss the Dimension 1 questions in the study book.

1. The poor are to be fed from the "gleanings of [the] harvest," the fruit and grain that is left after the harvesters gather the crop and the fruit and grain that falls on the ground.
2. Individuals are responsible to "love your neighbor as yourself," not to bear a grudge, and to "reprove your neighbor" or be found guilty yourself. (See how Jesus used this passage to describe the greatest commandment in Matthew 22:34–40.)
3. The Israelites are to treat foreigners who live in Israel as well as they treat their native-born neighbors. They

should do this in remembrance of the time they were foreigners in Egypt.
4. In the seventh year the people are not to cultivate the land nor are they to plant any crops. The land is to be given complete rest.

(B) Point out that the words of Leviticus 25:10 (in the King James Version) appear on the Liberty Bell.

● Ask the class to listen to Leviticus 25:10 and try to recall where they might have heard some of those words. Read the entire verse aloud, preferably from the King James Version.

● Discuss whether the words lost their true meaning when they were taken out of their context and inscribed on the Liberty Bell.

● Ask, "Why is there no reference to the year of jubilee anywhere in the words the 'founding fathers' of the United States chose to use on the Liberty Bell?" (The last part of the verse in the Bible mentions "jubilee.")

Dimension 2:
What Does the Bible Mean?

(C) Look at whether it is, or would have been, possible to observe jubilee.

- Make two headings on the board:
—Jubilee Advantages
—Jubilee Disadvantages
- Ask the class to read Leviticus 25:8-17, 28-33, 53-55 concerning the jubilee year. List the pros and cons for Israel in carrying out this legislation to the letter.

(D) Compare the biblical "sabbath year" and the weekly "sabbath day."

- Read Leviticus 25:1-7, 18-24. See which items would also apply to the proposed sabbath year. Add to the list in "C" whatever items would be appropriate concerning the sabbath year.
- Finally, ask which pieces would also fit the weekly sabbath observance. Again, add items to the list as necessary.

Dimension 3:
What Does the Bible Mean to Us?

(E) Encourage reports from last chapter.

- Recalling the last chapter's material, ask if anyone would like to share the results of making amends with someone. (See item "I," page 45.)

(F) Study a hymn.

- Have hymnals available for everyone and turn to "Blow Ye the Trumpet, Blow," (No. 379 in *The United Methodist Hymnal*). Depending on the size of the class, divide into two, three, or six groups with each group looking at three stanzas, two stanzas, or one stanza of the hymn.
—Ask group members to match up specific verses of Leviticus 25 with the words of the hymn.
—Note the lines that refer to Jesus. In what way is this a continuation of Leviticus 25?
- Does Jesus' coming mean the expiration of the Leviticus 25 ideas?

(G) Consider familiar words from Leviticus 19:18.

- Use of "love your neighbor as yourself" in literature:
  a. Parson: "soothly the lawe of God is the love of God" (Chaucer, *The Canterbury Tales*, "The Parson's Tale," 10.127).
  b. "the love of God principal, and loving of his neighebor as him-self" is the "remedie agayns this foule synne of Envye" (10.514).
- "Fractured" versions:
  a. Print Leviticus 19:18 on a large sheet of newsprint
  b. Print a "fractured" version at the top of other pieces of newsprint. For instance:
     "Do unto your neighbor before he does unto you."
     "The Golden Rule is: The one who has the gold makes the rules."
     (Parents of elementary school children may have heard other versions that can be added.)
  c. Have a supply of newspapers and magazines and either glue or tape on hand. Ask class members to cut out pictures, headlines, and so forth, and put them under the appropriate wording.
  d. If one "fractured" version is pictured more often, what might that say about our society?

(H) Discuss Jesus' two great commandments.

- Divide the class into three groups and have each read one of the following passages:
  —Matthew 22:34-40
  —Mark 12:28-34
  —Luke 10:25-28
  a. What is the response to Jesus' statement?
  b. Which response seems more likely?
  c. It appears that the lawyer in Luke is asking the question about the identity of the neighbor in the sense of "Who is the one who comes under the definition so that I have to help?" meaning "What is the definition of the person I am responsible for, so that I will know those I can safely ignore?"
  —Is this the question Jesus answers with the parable?
  —What is the relationship between the lawyer's question and Leviticus 19:18?
  —How does Jesus' answer correspond with Leviticus 19:18?

(I) Ask individuals to make lists.

- List types of people it is easy to consider neighbors.
- List types it is hard to feel neighborly about.

- Compare the lists and see if the class can come up with reasons or traits that put groups or individuals in one list rather than the other.
—What about a person's actions or attitudes may make us think "neighbor" on first meeting?
—List things within our own histories, both individual and communal, that may make it hard for us to accept certain individuals and groups as "neighbor."
—List anything about ourselves that could make it hard or impossible for others who see us to immediately think "neighbor."
- Which items in our own history (above) are under our control? What about other items listed above?
- Are there some things on the list that cannot be changed? A person's race or gender, for instance, is a fact the individual has no control over, unlike a surly attitude or vicious tongue.
—Mark those items that are the responsibility of the "viewer" of the individual rather than the individual.
- Ask class members to study the lists quietly for a few minutes and to think of something they can do in the following week to change that trait. If any are willing to share out loud, have them do so.

(J) Consider treatment of neighbors and strangers.

Certain regions of the country have stereotyped identities about their cuisine, their manners, and how long it takes a newcomer to "belong." Some towns are known as very neighborly. In others it is said that unless your family has lived there "since Moses was a boy" you are not a real member. What is the reputation of the region and the town you live in?

Denominations and individual churches also have similar reputations. Certain groups are called "cold" while others are "warm and friendly." Interestingly, the same labels seem to be attached to different denominations in different parts of the country.

- Make two lists, one headed "neighborly" and the other "like strangers." Ask the class members to call out attitudes, words, and specific ways of treating people they feel are appropriate under each heading.
- Focus now on the church. Are church members supposed to act like neighbors to one another? If so, what does that look like? Specifically, does it mean that things are always supposed to be cheerful and upbeat, welcoming and warm?

(K) Consider Jubilee Year and today.

- Return to the lists made in "C."
- How would the lists change if, instead of applying the legislation to ancient Israel, it were applied to contemporary Christians?
- Since the United States does not have one established religion, which provisions could not be applied to everyone? Which provisions would it be possible to apply?
- Are there ways in which the Jubilee Year legislation might be applied within the church? Since United Methodism is a connectional system, are there provisions that could be carried out in our church life, even if not in the civil sphere?
- What Jubilee Year provisions might an individual congregation live out?
- What portions of the Jubilee Year could an individual Christian fulfill?

(L) Look for a gleaning project.

- See if there are any gleaning projects in your area. Perhaps a representative would like to come and speak with your class.

    In one of my former charges, we had a produce table in the narthex. On Sunday mornings, people brought extra produce from their gardens and put it on the table. Others took whatever they wanted and left a money donation in a basket on the table. The money was collected and at the end of the summer sent to an Advance Special. During the summer the table had fruits, vegetables, and herbs. Most weeks there were flowers as well as edibles. Sometimes people brought homemade baked goods. It was a real treat for all of us, even without taking the money into consideration.

- For people without backyard gardens, let alone fields and vineyards, what can gleaning look like? Or are these sharing rules only for real estate owners? Brainstorm with the class members what you could make available for others to glean. Would a rummage sale qualify? Why, or why not?

(M) Solve the commandment puzzle.

- You will need scratch paper and pencils or pens for this activity.
- List the Ten Commandments in abbreviated form on board or newsprint. Divide the class into teams of two, and have each team look for a corresponding law for each commandment in Leviticus 19:3–20:10. Let them write their answers on scratch paper. (Possible answers are given in brackets.)

1. No other gods. [Leviticus 19:4]
2. No idols. [Leviticus 19:3]
3. No misuse of God's name. [Leviticus 19:12]
4. Keep the sabbath. [Leviticus 19:3]
5. Honor parents. [Leviticus 19:3]
6. Do not murder. [Leviticus 19:16]
7. Do not commit adultery. [Leviticus 20:10]
8. Do not steal. [Leviticus 19:11]
9. No false witness. [Leviticus 19:16]
10. Do not covet. [Leviticus 19:18]

(Some commandments have more than one correct answer.)

Let the teams compete in supplying all the answers.

- Come back together as a whole group and write answers next your list on the board or newsprint.

(N) Puzzle out commandments.

- This is the same sort of exercise as "M," but the other way round. Begin with Leviticus 19:3-4, 9-18, and 30-37 and decide which of the Ten Commandments is involved in each case. Make a chart and see which commandments have many references and which have few or even none. What might that tell us about what was important for Israel?

(O) "Rewrite" some rules.

- In groups of two or three, ask class members to rewrite Leviticus 19:17-18

—in contemporary language, trying to keep the same meaning;

—in whatever the opposite of Leviticus 19:17-18 would be;

—in a "version with training wheels." That is, write the rules for someone who wants eventually to be able to live up to the Leviticus version but who does not feel able to do it all at once;

—in different versions for specific groups. Try your hand at some of the following. (The point is to try to use wording that will have the same ultimate meaning as the biblical text, but that will take into consideration the specific circumstances of each particular group.)

    a. a man's version.
    b. a woman's version
    c. a children's version
    d. a version for small towns
    e. a version for big cities
    f. a version for people who live alone
    g. a personal, private version that each class member can write individually to suit his or her own circumstances.

(P) Plan a time of reflection.

- About five minutes before the end of the class period, ask each person to reflect on what has gone on during the hour. Go around the room and ask each person to mention one thing he or she will continue to think about during the coming week.

Additional Bible Helps

Sabbath, Sabbath Year, and Jubilee Year

Leviticus 25 is a summing up of legislation that occurs throughout the Torah. These laws look in two directions at once. First, they show how things ought to be, how God would like them to be, for the sake of the whole creation. But they are not "pie in the sky" or "utopian" texts, because they recognize the presence and power of sin in the world. This is seen clearly in their second direction. By listing ways the people are to get back to the intended circumstances when they are lost, these laws recognize that things do not always go as intended. The basic reasoning goes like this:

1. There should not be any poor people in the land. If everyone lives according to the covenant, there won't be any poor.
2. But in case there are any poor people (which will mean that some folks are no longer following the covenant), the needs of the poor are to be met generously.
   a. Immediate needs (food, clothing, shelter) are to be met by family and neighbors.
   b. Mid-term needs (having had to sell their land, for instance and so having nowhere to grow food or pasture animals) are also met by the extended family in terms of the "redemption" of the land.
   c. Long-term needs cannot be met by the kinship system alone but require "political" action also. The biblical term is "release" to describe the long-term responses to landlessness and indentured servitude. This "release" means the total change, the restoration, of the political arrangements so that there will not be poverty again.
3. If the items under 2 are taken care of, then the LORD will be honored. Actually, if 2a and 2b were taken care of, then 2c would not be needed at all. What God set up in the Sinai covenant was a covenantal egalitarian society. What sin pushes humans toward is an aristocratic/peasant society. Because of those pushes and pressures, there is legislation such as that of Leviticus 25 that attempts to keep the skewed arrangements from becoming permanent.

Did the sabbath year ever happen, let alone the celebration of a jubilee year? We cannot be sure, but there is some indication that something in that direction actually did take place. There are a couple of hints from late periods in Israel's history. Jeremiah 34 relates what happened under King Zedekiah, between the two Babylonian deportations. It seems that some people took to heart the disaster and repented. They even began to live out some of the legislation, including that of the sabbath and jubilee years. However, it was a cynical and calculating "repentance" in name only; and the landowners and slaveholders soon reclaimed their property. You can read about this in Jeremiah 34:8-22.

Nehemiah 10 comes from the postexilic period, when some people had returned to the ruined Jerusalem from Babylon. They reaffirm their promise to live by the covenant and refer to some of the specific laws they mean to honor. The verse that interests us here is 31b: "we will forego the crops of the seventh year and the exaction of every debt."

First Maccabees 6:49, 53, which is from a still later period, mentions the sabbatical year, almost in passing.

Although the evidence is meager, to be sure, these arrangements were taken seriously enough that they are remembered and referred to as late as the time of the Maccabees. Perhaps that is the best we humans can do: keep an ideal out there ahead of us.

11

Numbers
11:4-16;
12:1–13:3
13:25–14:9

*I*S THE HAND OF THE LORD SHORT?

LEARNING MENU

Keeping in mind the ways your class members learn best, as well as their needs and interests, choose at least one learning segment from each of the three Dimensions.

Dimension 1:
What Does the Bible Say?

(A) Answer the Dimension 1 questions in the study book.

Question 1 is answered by a wishful grocery list. Your class might discuss the problems a large band of people on the move would have in securing the various types of food named in Numbers 11:5. Compared to a settled population, even a population of slaves, the Israelites in the wilderness could have found neither fish nor vegetables readily available.

Question 3 is a good example of a disguised conflict. Aaron and Miriam complain about Moses' wife, "a Cushite woman." (The KJV calls her Ethiopian.) We have had no reference to Zipporah, the wife introduced in Exodus 2:21, since Exodus 18. Was she no longer living when

Moses married the "Cushite"? Or had Moses remained separated from her when her father Jethro brought her back to where the Israelites were camped (Exodus 18:2-7, 27)? These questions are left unanswered as the text quickly moves to the jealousy his sister and brother feel toward Moses.

(B) Recollect and appreciate a threefold benediction.

In Numbers 6:22-27 a blessing widely known and often memorized by Christians and Jews can be found.

● Divide your class into three groups, with one group reading verse 24, another reading verse 25, and the third reading verse 26. Review again the learning about "God's Name," (study book, page 16; or this leader's guide, page 12).

● Ask class members to tell if these verses are familiar to them. What do the verses bring to mind? (Many people who were part of the United Methodist Youth Fellowship [UMYF] as youth will recall these verses as the benediction used by that group.)

—Ask, "How many persons were surprised to learn that this benediction comes from the Book of Numbers?"

Dimension 2:
What Does the Bible Mean?

(C) Consider people's attitudes toward food.

● Ask any class members to volunteer to describe what it felt like on an occasion when they were very hungry.

● Still remembering that time of hunger, ask what food they would have been willing to eat under those conditions. The likelihood is that a really hungry person will eat with gratitude any food that is available. Hunger pangs can make anything taste good!

● Now turn to Numbers 11:4-6 and have someone read it aloud.

—Does this sound like people on the verge of starvation?
—What does this say about God's care for the people?
—What does it say about the people's response to or appreciation of that care?

● Call attention to Numbers 11:8 as an indication that the Israelites had learned ways to prepare manna, perhaps to improve the taste.

(D) Discuss the dispute between Moses and his sister and brother.

● What is the dispute in Exodus 12:1-9 really about? Are Aaron and Miriam arguing primarily about Moses' wife or about their feeling left out of the leadership roles they think should be theirs?

● Does God respond to the complaint about Moses' wife? Is this another indication of what the issue truly is?

● Ask the class members for examples they have witnessed, or participated in, where the real reason for a dispute was not what was being argued about on the surface.

● Do you think the issue would have been resolved had Aaron and Miriam confined their words to discussing Moses' wife? What does that say about our arguments today?

● Why was only Miriam "punished" for disputing with Moses (12:10-16)?

Dimension 3:
What Does the Bible Mean to Us?

(E) Consider the implications of Miriam's disease that followed her dispute with Moses.

● Familiarize class members with the incident by reading aloud Numbers 12:4-15.

● It is well known now that what is called leprosy in the Bible is not the same disease that goes by that name today (also known as Hansen's disease). The actual physical malady, however, is not the point of Numbers 12. Ask class members to list the important features of the disease in this text. Be sure to include

  a. It was visible to all.

  b. It was immediately assumed to be a punishment (Numbers 12:11).

  c. It forced Miriam's exclusion from the camp.

  If there is a surprise in this story, it is that all Israel waited the seven days until Miriam could come back into the camp (Numbers 12:15).

● Discuss how *leper* has come to have a figurative meaning in our culture. Ask for examples of how this term is used today, with a nonmedical meaning.

● AIDS is sometimes called the "modern leprosy."

—Which of the characteristics of this story as noted above fit AIDS and which do not?
—What would be a comparable action by society today to correspond with the people's waiting for Miriam's return to the camp?

(F) Examine how meanings change with context.

Often the context in which a statement occurs will add meaning or change the meaning of that statement from its bare dictionary definitions. To understand what is being said we need to know not only the dictionary definitions of the words, but also the setting in which the words are spoken.

● Ask for two volunteers to read the following dialogue (adapted from a moderately famous example in the field of linguistics).

  Man: I have two canaries.
  Woman: That's nice.
  Man: I also have a son.
  Woman: Oh, I'm sorry.

54

JOURNEY THROUGH THE BIBLE

- Ask the class members, in groups of three or four, to discuss the possible meanings of the woman's second response.

  a. Maybe she means that children are more trouble to take care of than pets.

  b. Maybe she is simply not paying any attention to what he is saying and so really doesn't even know what she is saying.

  c. Maybe . . . (Fill in the blank.)

- Then give them this context: the woman is an apartment superintendent and the man is inquiring about a vacancy. The building allows caged birds but not children.

- When class members see this idea of meanings-changed-by-context, return to Numbers 11–14.

- On newsprint, ask the class to list the major events of these chapters, chapter by chapter. Using Chapter 11 as an example, they might list:
—grumbling about food again
—Moses' complaint to God
—consecration of seventy elders
—Eldad and Medad
—quails

- Make similar lists for Chapters 12, 13, and 14.

- Divide the class into four groups and assign each group one chapter. Cut apart the events in each chapter and "shuffle" them. Ask groups to see what meanings they can come up with by putting events in different order. In Chapter 11 for instance, what would it mean if the grumbling about food had been followed immediately by the quails, without the consecration of the elders in between?

- After each group looks at alternative arrangements, have them put the events back in biblical order and see what new insights they have about the meanings of their chapter.

- Finally, as a whole class, do the same thing with the chapters themselves: what do we learn by having the events of Chapter 14 precede those of Chapter 12, and so forth.

(G) Consider the place of gender in the complaints.

- Ask for volunteers to play Miriam, Aaron, and Moses and "act out" Numbers 12:1-2. Since there is very little direct speech in the text, they will need to improvise.

- Next, repeat the scene, but this time have Miriam and Moses complain about Aaron's wife.

- Although we are not told whether Miriam is married, for the sake of this exercise assume that she is. Ask the players—or new volunteers—to have Moses and Aaron complain about Miriam's husband.

- As a whole class, discuss these issues after the play-acting:
—How many assumptions do we make—about the legitimacy of the complaint for example—according to the gender of the participants?
—Similarly, what assumptions do we make based on the status, age, role, or title of the participants?
—What can we learn about assumptions we make in our relationships?

(H) Send some "spies" outside the classroom.

- Ask class members to pretend they are on a long journey to a place none has been before. Send two or three "spies" out of the room to find out what lies ahead. Ask each "spy" to be ready to describe or bring back something that symbolizes what they found outside the room. Depending on weather and other circumstances, they may want to bring back something signifying the conditions and any growing vegetation outside the building too. (See Numbers 13:23.)

- When the "spies" return with their symbolic objects and/or reports, let class members decide if these are positive or negative signs of what lies before them.

- Ask for a vote on whether the group should move to the place described or remain in their comfortable current location.

- Turn your discussion then to the reaction of the Israelites to what their own spies brought to them. For example, might a cluster of grapes so big it had to be carried on a pole between two men (Numbers 13:23) indeed signify the land was inhabited by giants?

(I) Decide where you are going.

- Ask each individual to bring in for next week's class some symbol of his or her own "Promised Land" and tell of a hoped-for destination.

(J) Apply Israel's missed opportunity to our lives.

- Remind the class members of what happens at the end of Chapter 14: After the people refuse to cross over into the Promised Land, saying yet again that they would rather return to the safety and security of Egypt, and Moses relays to them God's decision that they will not cross into the Land, **then** they decide to do it. Despite Moses' warning that they will be defeated, they go ahead. And they are defeated. But they say before going that they know they have sinned (Numbers 14:40).

- Questions for discussion:
—Is it fair of God to allow the people to be defeated after they acknowledge their sin?
—Is it ever too late to do what God requests?
—Does God's refusal to let that generation cross over into the Promised Land mean God broke the promise made to them when they left Egypt?

- Ask for volunteers to tell of an experience when they changed their mind about something but it was too late to do or have the original thing. Or perhaps they have been the one to tell someone else—a friend, a child, a spouse—that what was offered and refused is now no longer available.
—How does it feel to realize what was available before is no longer available because of one's indecision or wrong decision?
—How does it feel to deny other persons something they dearly want, even though they had given some indication they did not want it after all?

- What do these human experiences have to say about our relationship to God? Is it ever too late to repent and accept forgiveness of sins?

(K) Read aloud quotations to spark discussion.

- Here is another view of the conflict between Miriam and Moses' wife, assumed in this case to be Zipporah.

"Miriam was very unhappy at sight of Zipporah. She knew that all the feminine eyes of Israel saw the wife of Moses just as she did. They were bound to be impressed and to fall in behind her if she but beckoned. Miriam looked at her own rough clothing which was hung with jewelry that had been taken in battle, then turned her eyes away from the fine raiment of the woman on the camel. She looked again and saw well-cared-for hands and feet of Zipporah, and looked at her own gnarled fists and her square feet all twisted and coarsened by slavery, and almost snarled out loud. She, Miriam, had had so little in her life and now this place she had won by hard work and chance was being taken from her by the looks of a Prince's daughter who hadn't done anything but deck herself to come here and bewitch the eyes of foolish women! Miriam boiled with anger and a sense of injustice. So she snarled and said things to the women about her.

" 'Look at the hussy! Look what is getting down off that camel, will you! Somebody to come queen it over us poor people and rob us. Look at her trying to look like Mrs. Pharaoh! That Moses and his tricks. Fooling me and Aaron to do all the hard work for him down in Egypt and telling us all he meant to do for us as soon as he got to Sinai. Then soon as he got here, before he can talk to God, he got to send for that woman to put her over me! I'll show him. I'll show her too. I don't aim to be robbed out of my labor like that. Just look at her— the way she walks' " (from *Moses: Man of the Mountain*, by Zora Neale Hurston; University of Illinois Press, 1984; pages 269–70).

- We may miss many of the references and allusions to biblical stories that poets and other authors put in their work. At the time John Greenleaf Whittier wrote, a higher proportion of the general population knew more Bible stories than the general population does today. Knowing and not-knowing the story he is referring to may make a difference in the enjoyment of the poem. Here are a few lines from Whittier's "The Fruit-gift":

"Thrilled with a glad surprise, methought I knew
The pleasure of the homeward-turning Jew
When Eschol's clusters on his shoulders lay,*
Dropping their sweetness on his desert way."

* See Numbers 13:23.

- Much earlier than Whittier is Chaucer's *The Canterbury Tales*. In them, the Summoner is described as follows:
"Wel loved he garleek, onyons, and eek lekes,
And for to drinken strong wyn, reed as blood."
 (1.634-35)

 Even if reading a modern language version that spells "garlic, onions, and leeks" and "red wine" the way we do, do you think many people today would understand the reference to Numbers 11? Does it make a difference in your view of the character to realize that Chaucer is describing him as the Israelites in Numbers 11?

(L) Share in closing reflections from today's session.

- About five minutes before the end of the class period, ask each person to reflect on what has gone on during the hour. Go around the room and ask each person to mention one thing he or she will continue to think about during the coming week.

- Use the benediction from "B" (Numbers 6:24-26) for your closing prayer.

Additional Bible Helps

Numbers/Bemidbar

The Book of Numbers in Hebrew is called *Bemidbar*, which means "in the wilderness." As in the cases of Exodus/Names and Leviticus/And-he-called, this name is used because Bemidbar/In-the-wilderness is the first significant word of the book. It also is a good description of the content of the book, referring not only to the Israelites' physical location, but to their "spiritual geography" as well. These chapters, 11–14, point this up well. They also present the only stated reason for the Israelites' spending forty years in the wilderness before finally entering the Promised Land.

Who Were the Rabble?

Numbers 11:4 in the RSV and the NRSV introduces a word that divides the migrating people into two groups. "*The rabble* . . . had a strong craving; *and the Israelites* wept again and said, 'If only we had meat to eat!' " (italics added). As they list a menu of foods they remember from Egypt (verse 5) fish is mentioned, but no meat.

Probably there were nomad families and individuals who had lived alone until, welcomed or not, they found the large group and decided to travel with them. The word *rabble* is defined as a class or group of people regarded with contempt.

Compared with other translations "rabble" seems to be an emotion-laden word. *Today's English Version* says, "There were foreigners traveling with the Israelites." The *Revised English Bible* says, "A mixed company of strangers had joined the Israelites."

We need to go back briefly to Leviticus 19:33-34 and read, "When an alien resides with you in your land, you shall not oppress the alien. The alien who resides with you shall be to you as the citizen among you; you shall love the alien as yourself, for you were aliens in the land of Egypt: I am the LORD your God."

12

Deuteronomy 6

ISRAELITES— THE NEXT GENERATION

Dimension 1:
What Does the Bible Say?

(A) Everyone echo a single reader.

- Using Deuteronomy 9:6-7 select someone to read the words and put into action the motions below:

Know then that the LORD your God
(entire group repeats)
is not giving you this good land
(repeat)
to occupy because of your righteousness;
(leader folds arms across chest as class repeats)
for you are a stubborn people.
(leader shakes finger at class; they repeat)
Remember and do not forget
(touch finger to head; class repeats)

how you provoked the LORD your God
(repeat)
to wrath in the wilderness
(repeat)
you have been rebellious against the LORD
(shake finger)
from the day you came out of the land of Egypt
(repeat)
until you came to this place.
(repeat)

(B) Answer the Dimension 1 questions in the study book.

- If the class finds Question 1 puzzling, point out in Deuteronomy 6:2-3 a series of "so thats." Israel is to keep God's laws so that God may be feared by the current and future generations, so that their days may be long, so that it may go well with them, and so that they may "multiply greatly."

- Ask individuals who have found answers to the other questions to share them with the class.

Dimension 2:
What Does the Bible Mean?

(C) Write "body parts" sentences.

● List the following body parts on the board or newsprint:

nose	thumb
head	foot
brain	mouth

● Divide the class into two teams and ask each to come up with a list of sentences using these different body parts in a figurative way. For example, "Toni has a real head for numbers" or "That applause has given Toni a swelled head."

● Next, see how many other body parts each team can find with figurative, symbolic uses in English speech.

● If anyone in the group has another language for a first language, ask for examples of how names of body parts are used differently in that language.

● Use this exercise as a lead-in to discussion of "heart" as it is used in Deuteronomy 6:5. Help class members see that words can have different symbolic meanings in the same language even when they refer to the same object.

(D) Pretend to be five again.

The Promised Land has been described many times as a land "flowing with milk and honey." It is described that way again in this chapter's text (verse 3).

● Ask each person to choose a partner. Ask them to imagine they are all five-year-olds and tell their partner what a land "flowing with milk and honey" would be like.

● Then ask them to think of themselves as the parent or babysitter of five-year-old twins. Tell them, "Now describe to your five-year-olds what 'flowing with milk and honey' might sound like to you."

● Tell everyone they may be "five" or may return to their own ages for the next questions.

—Is "flowing with milk and honey" a description of how things will be every day, or only on special occasions?

—If it is every day, is that the same as saying every day will be a party day?

—What two words would you use to describe your life now?

—What two words would describe how you would like your life to be?

Dimension 3:
What Does the Bible Mean to Us?

(E) Examine symbols of personal "Promised Lands."

● By way of review from last session, ask if any of the class members have brought in items that symbolize the "Promised Land" for them.

● Offer time for sharing by those who have brought things.

(F) Practice different ways of saying the same words.

● Divide class members into pairs.

● Have each pair take turns saying "I love you" to each other in as many different ways as they can think of. This will probably include the off-hand sentence at the end of a telephone conversation, the gritted-teeth words demanded by parents that siblings say to each other after a squabble, and other ways that class members can come up with.

● Next ask them to see if they can find different ways to say, "I love God."

—Do some feel appropriate and others inappropriate?
—What makes the difference?

● Relate these observations to the command to love God in Deuteronomy 6:5.

(G) Make "doorposts" and other reminders for the home.

● You will need a supply of paper in different colors, crayons, pens, markers, and other art materials.

● After a discussion of Deuteronomy 6:5-9, 20-24, ask people to suggest what would serve as a reminder to them in their own houses. Some may think of a framed needlepoint motto or a mezuzah like Jewish neighbors may have. (Mezuzah: "a small piece of parchment inscribed with . . . Deuteronomy 6:5-9 and 11:13-21 and marked with the word *Shaddai*, a name of the Almighty, that is rolled up in a container and affixed by many Jewish households to their door frames in conformity with Jewish law and as a sign of their faith"—*American Heritage Dictionary*, Third Edition, 1992).

● Using the supplies available, let class members make a sign, marker, Bible verse, or whatever will serve the same purpose for them as the words on the doorposts in Deuteronomy 6.

(H) Talk about who helped with breakfast.

- Make sure everyone has paper and pencil.

- Ask them to list two things they have done this day, such as shower, eat breakfast, drive to church, read the newspaper.

- For each item, list how many other people were involved.

- Share findings with the entire class.

  People who live alone may very well say no one else was involved in what they did, while people in families may count only the other members of their household. Push them to think farther:

—Did you pump your own wash water this morning? In some areas, people must do that task for themselves.

—Did you cook your breakfast over a campfire you made yourself? from wood you cut yourself? In some places, people do.

- Write "breakfast" on the center of a piece of newsprint or on the board.

—Ask people to call out what they ate. Write the items with plenty of space around them.

—For each item, ask where it came from and who else was involved in getting it to the breakfast table. Again in some cases, the individual may have done it all: grew and picked and washed and ate a peach, for instance. For most cases, however, there will be a multitude of other people, known and unknown, who had something to do with getting our breakfast to us.

- Is Deuteronomy 6:10-15 telling us to remember to thank God for what we have? Is there anything about our relationship to other people? After all, the folks who built the houses and planted the vineyards and made all the things the Israelites were going to take over were Canaanites who were going to be forcibly evicted—or killed—as the Israelites advanced. Does this mean that gratitude is due only to God?

(I) Retell the story.

Since Deuteronomy is in the form of Moses' telling a new generation the story of the Exodus, Sinai, and wilderness wanderings all over again, make your own versions.

- Divide into three groups. Let each group prepare the story of this study of Exodus through Deuteronomy for a different audience:

—elementary school children;

—teenagers who have grown up in the church;

—adults with no particular Christian or biblical background.

- Urge the groups not to rely on spoken words alone. Use

music, body movement, colors, group participation, and so forth. Try to condense the material into a five-minute presentation.

- Leave time for each group to present its version of the story. The "audience" in each case should try to listen and participate as if they really were elementary-age school children, teenagers, or whatever target audience they represent.

- After the presentations, point out similar elements each group included and where they differed.

—Is there a central core of the story that cannot be eliminated?

—Are some things more appropriate for one age group or background than another?

(J) Interview others to see how well our biblical history is being handed down.

- If your class meets at a time and place where there are other age groups meeting, seek the cooperation of the other teachers and classes. Send interviewing teams to ask the other classes a uniform list of a few questions, such as:

—Who was Moses?

—What happened at Mount Sinai?

—What was the Exodus?

- After conducting the interviews, have the groups report and compare results.

(K) Consider how jewelry is used symbolically.

- Ask for a show of hands of class members who are wearing a cross around their neck or other jewelry or emblems with religious symbols.

- Ask class members to tell what wearing such symbols means to them.

—Do they intend their message primarily as a reminder for themselves or for other people who may see the symbols? Is it perhaps a conversation-starter?

—Have they ever thought of it before in terms of Deuteronomy 6:8?

- If there is a Conservative or Reform Jewish congregation in the vicinity, perhaps you can invite one of the men to come and show the group his phylacteries or tefillin.

  These are small leather boxes that hold strips of parchment with Scripture verses on them; They are worn on the left arm and forehead during morning worship. Orthodox Jews wear them also, but their tradition would discourage meeting with a Christian group, especially with women present. While some Orthodox Jews may be quite willing, if there are other options available it would be better not to put someone in an uncomfortable position.

(L) Review the Deuteronomy version of the commandments.

Deuteronomy 5:6-21 is a repetition of the commandments found in Exodus 20:1-17.

● Divide the class into three groups.

—Group 1 is to compare the two versions of the sabbath commandment (Exodus 20:8-11; Deuteronomy 5:12-15).

—Group 2 is to compare the coveting commandment, noticing in particular the relative positions of "house" and "wife" (Exodus 20:17; Deuteronomy 5:21).

—Group 3 is to compare the other eight commandments.

● What similarities and differences do they find? Are the differences substantial in terms of meaning or do they seem to be stylistic only?

(M) Discuss a midrash on the forty years of wandering.

● Read aloud the following midrash. Ask class members to listen for anything they may hear that surprises them.

"For forty years the Holy One made Israel go in a roundabout way through the wilderness, saying, 'Should I now lead them on a straight route, each one will take possession of a field or a vineyard and regard himself as not obligated to study Torah. I shall therefore lead them by way of the wilderness, where they will eat manna, drink the waters of the well, and so [give themselves to the study of] Torah, which will then be inculcated in them.' Moreover, when the Canaanites heard that Israel was about to enter the Land, they burned the newly planted seeds, uprooted trees, cut down saplings, demolished buildings, and stopped up wells. The Holy One said: I promised Abraham to bring his children into a land full of good things. So I shall detain them for forty years in the wilderness, until the Canaanites get busy and repair what they have damaged" (quoted in *The Book of Legends: Sefer Ha-Aggadah*, edited by Hayim Nahman Bialik and Yehoshua Hana Ravnitzky, translated by William G. Braude; Schocken Books, 1992; pages 99–100).

(N) Take time to reflect.

● About five minutes before the end of the class period, ask each person to reflect on what has gone on during the hour. Go around the room and ask them to say one thing they will ponder during the coming week.

Additional Bible Helps

"Deuteronomy"
Both in standard English and in literally translated Hebrew the Book of Deuteronomy begins: "These are the words that Moses spoke to all Israel beyond the Jordan." Thus in Hebrew the book is know as *Devarim* or "Words."

Our word *Deuteronomy* is derived from the Greek, coming from "deutero-"/second and "nomos"/law. The "second" of course refers to the second time through the telling of the story and not an additional set of legal materials.

Translating the "Shema"
After the address, "Hear, O Israel," there are only four words in Hebrew for the "Shema" (shuh-MAH). Transliterated literally they are:

> the-Lord
> our-God
> the-Lord
> one

By the plain rules of grammar, an appropriate form of "to be" can be placed between any of the words. This yields the following translations:

> (1) The Lord is our God, the one Lord.
> (2) The Lord is our God, the Lord is one.
> (3) The Lord our God, the Lord is one.

Since the word translated "one" has often been rendered "alone" in this verse, we also have

> (4) The Lord is our God, the Lord alone.
> (5) The Lord our God is Lord alone.

Most English translations choose one or another of these—with some slight variations—for the main text and often put one or more as marginal notes.

Which one is right? In a case like this, that is a less helpful question than "what do they mean?" (There is plenty of scholarly discussion, not only in commentaries on Deuteronomy, but also in articles and monographs on this one verse. Most of it, however, is very technical and turns on the details and peculiarities of biblical Hebrew.)

In terms of meaning, these five renderings fall into two categories. They focus either on the relationship of Israel and God ("The Lord is our God") or on Lord-ly characteristics ("The Lord is one"). Both categories of meaning are clearly biblical. There is never any question that God wants to have a close relationship with Israel, desires to be thought of as "our God." Neither is there ever any doubt that there are no other gods worth thinking about. (You may wish to refer again to "henotheism"—the belief in one god without denying the existence of other gods—in the discussion of the first commandment, page 36.)

Perhaps Hebrew has the advantage over English in this case. The Hebrew sentence can have both those meanings simultaneously, whereas English has to choose between them.

More on the Commandments

Learning activity "L" involves comparing the Exodus and Deuteronomy versions of the Ten Commandments. A substantial difference occurs with regard to the reason given for keeping the sabbath. According to Exodus it is because God worked for six days to create the world and rested on day seven. Therefore, people are to imitate God and rest.

In Deuteronomy, however, nothing at all is said about creation. Instead, the Israelites are reminded that they were slaves in Egypt and that God freed them from slavery. Therefore, they are supposed to keep the sabbath.

As usual, the question to be asked is not "which version is correct?" but "what do we learn from each version?" Several possibilities come to mind.

- If the reasons were reversed—slavery in Exodus and creation in Deuteronomy—there would not be the repeated telling of the commandments as there is now. The people in Deuteronomy are not, literally, the ones who were slaves, so perhaps they need this reminder more than the previous generation.

- Is freedom from slavery just something to be remembered from the past? Not at all. The people of Israel are to remember that God did not like it when the Egyptians enslaved them. The implication is clear: God will not like it if they enslave anyone else. Not even "slaves" are to be treated as the Egyptians treated the Israelites. Implied in the wording is the promise that as God freed one set of slaves, God can free others if the need arises.

- The creation connection in Exodus gives a positive reason for the sabbath observance. Sabbath is not just "rest from" but also "rest for." One rests from regular work in order to have time for the joy of creation. God rested on the seventh day not out of weariness, but in order to delight in what had just been made. Similarly, people are to take time to enjoy the fruits of their labors—or to "stop and smell the roses" in popular terminology.

13

Deuteronomy
26:1-11, 16-19;
30:11-20; 34:1-12

THAT WAS THEN; THIS IS NOW

LEARNING MENU

Keeping in mind the ways your class members learn best, as well as their needs and interests, choose at least one learning segment from each of the three Dimensions.

Dimension 1:
What Does the Bible Say?

(A) Answer the Dimension 1 questions in the study book.

1. These verses tell in a few words the history of the Israelites, from the "wandering Aramean" going to Egypt to the people being enslaved, saved by God, and given a land "flowing with milk and honey."

2. By obeying God's statutes and ordinances, the Israelites will be God's special people, "holy to the LORD your God."

3. God's requirements are "not too hard" for the people. God's word is "very near; . . . in your mouth and in your heart for you to observe."

4. At the end of the Book of Deuteronomy, the Israelites

are in Moab, southeast of Canaan. They have not yet entered the Promised Land.

(B) Look at Moses through New Testament eyes.

● Acts 7:17-44 gives us the story of Moses as told by Stephen (in the forthright sermon that led to his death). A much briefer account of Moses' life "by faith" is found in Hebrews 11:23-29. Ask class members to read one or both of these passages, looking for well-stated expressions or new insights that they do not remember from Exodus, Leviticus, Numbers, or Deuteronomy.

Dimension 2:
What Does the Bible Mean?

(C) Discuss the meaning of anamnesis.

Anamnesis (an-am-NEE-sis) is a recalling to memory or a recollection.

● Go over the section in the study book, pages 104–105, about the generational leap between "our ancestors were slaves" and "the Lord freed us." Discuss the significance of that change from past tense ("our ancestors") to present tense ("us").

(D) Identify the "wandering Aramean."

- If anyone in the class has a Bible in the King James Version, ask that Deuteronomy 26:5 be read aloud. ("A Syrian ready to perish was my father, and he went down into Egypt, and sojourned there with a few, and became there a nation, great, mighty, and populous.")

- Discuss who among the ancestors of the Hebrew people "went down to Egypt." (Abraham had done so, but the reference to the growth of the Hebrew population clearly makes Jacob the "Syrian" or Aramean [in NRSV] referred to.)

    Biblical references to Syria and to Aram are using two names for the same place. Since Syria continues to be the name of a political state in the world today, the use of the term *Aramean* keeps our focus on patriarchal times.

Dimension 3:
What Does the Bible Mean to Us?

(E) Discover anamnesis in the family and the church.

- Ask two or three volunteers to tell the class a brief, pleasant anecdote about one of their grandparents, preferably from the grandparent's childhood or youth.
—How do they know that story?
—Have they told it to anyone?
—If they have children, do their children know this story? If so, why?

- Next, ask class members to think back to their earliest happy family memory.
—How do they remember that incident? (In some cases, they may not be sure if they actually remember the event, or simply remember having heard the story so many times that they think they remember it.)
—Have they told anyone about it?
—If they have children, have their children heard the story? If so, why?

- As a whole class, sing at least one verse of No. 288 in *The United Methodist Hymnal*, "Were You There When They Crucified My Lord?"

- Divide into groups of three or four persons. Ask each group to write another verse to that hymn, following the pattern of the other stanzas:

    "Were you there when _____."

    Suggest that each group use an incident or concern that is on their minds today.

Perhaps the class can sing the new stanzas together toward the end of the session, as a way of drawing the study to a close. Begin and end with the traditional verse 1, and sing the new verses in between.

(F) Consider Deuteronomy's "Little Creed."

Deuteronomy 26:5-9 has sometimes been called the "Little Creed," because of the way it seems to encapsulate and summarize much of the core Israelite faith.

- As a group, list the events this passage mentions.

- Are there any major events that have happened between the beginning of Exodus and the close of Deuteronomy that are not recited?

- If so, what does their omission mean? Must it mean that those events didn't happen? that the people don't believe in them? that they aren't important?

(G) Compare the Apostle's Creed and the "Little Creed."

- If you can, gather several copies of *The United Methodist Hymnal* for this session.

- In groups of three or four ask persons to read the Apostles' Creed, Nos. 881 and 882. (If hymnals are not available, write the Creed on the board or on newsprint ahead of time and have it posted where everyone can read it easily.)

- Ask groups to compare the Apostles' Creed and Deuteronomy 26:5-9. To what extent are they alike? In what ways do they differ?

    The words from Deuteronomy are to be recited in the context of a liturgy, a worship service that includes the offering of first fruits. Under what circumstances does your congregation say the Apostles' Creed? Note that it appears in *The United Methodist Hymnal* not only at Nos. 881 and 882 but also on pages 7, 35, 41, 46, and 51.

    In *The United Methodist Book of Worship* (1992), the Apostles' Creed is also mentioned within the Services of Death and Resurrection (page 149), Consecration of Diaconal Ministers (page 656), Ordination of Deacons (page 665) and Elders (page 674), the Consecration of Bishops (page 702), and the Service of Farewell to a Bishop or District Superintendent (page 732).

    What difference does the liturgical or ritual context make in the meaning of the creed? Might it be heard differently by the participants under different circumstances?

    Are we saying anything particular by the fact that this creed is specified for some services and not for others?

(H) Compare other creeds.

- In the same small groups look at other creeds that are widely used within Christianity.

- Compare these creeds to the Deuteronomy text, especially the Nicene Creed, No. 880 in *The United Methodist Hymnal*. List some differences and likenesses.

(I) Compose statements of faith.

- In the same small groups, ask each to compose a statement of faith. If there is time, the following items could lead to stimulating discussions before the groups begin work on actual composition of their creed. If time is limited however, you may wish simply to specify the answers to each, in terms of the exercise. Alternatively, answering these questions, and any others the groups come up with, could be part of the group's task.

—Will the statement of faith be general—such that it would be suitable for all Christians—or specific to your denomination?

—Will it be general in terms of historical time, or relate specifically to the present day?

—Will it be general in terms of the ages of those who say it, or specific to a particular time of life?

—Will it be general in terms of usage, or relate to a specific context—such as a Sunday school class, Bible study group, or to be used primarily within a Baptism service?

—Will there be a limit to its length?

(J) Put together views from the mountaintop.

- You will need newspapers and magazines that can be cut up, scissors, and tape or glue. Ask people to work in groups of two or three to make a collage of "views from the mountaintop into the Promised Land."

- Make a second collage, "views from the bottom of the mountain."

- Let each group share its pictures with the whole class. Discuss the differences in the views and what hinders us from moving from the "bottom" situation to that which is glimpsed from the mountaintop.

- How much of the mountaintop view may we legitimately work for in this life, and how much can come only in the next life?

- Is putting parts of the mountaintop view off to the next life a way of shirking responsibility for trying to better life in this world? Or is any talk at all of the next life a way of abandoning hope in this world? What are appro-

priate ways of balancing what only God can do and what humans are to do in faithful relationship to God?

(K) Make sight-unseen choices using brown bags.

- Have several small brown paper bags set up on a table at the front of the room. Each one should contain something different (see suggestions below). The bags should be closed so that the contents are not visible.
  a. cotton balls
  b. a sealed plastic bag of water (something to feel squishy without leaking through the paper bag)
  c. a candy bar
  d. pretty stones
  e. an aspirin tablet
  f. a banana, peach, or other fresh fruit
  g. a book of matches

- Put signs with the following wording attached to the appropriate bag ("a." sign goes with "a." bag, and so on).
  a. useful in some circumstances
  b. vital to life; can kill
  c. nice but dangerous to some
  d. pretty, but you can't eat them
  e. vital to some; deadly for others
  f. good today but may be yucky by next week
  g. useful; sometimes deadly

- Ask which bags people would be willing to have in their homes. People may feel them, shake them, and so forth, as long as they do not look inside.

- After everyone has decided, show the contents of each bag.

- Read Deuteronomy 30:15-20. Instead of telling them the point of the exercise, ask the class members themselves to make a connection between the text and the bag game. (Verses 19 and 20 contain one connection.)

(L) Use these quotations for discussion-starters.

- Use one or two biblical references in literature, where an author is depending on the reader's familiarity with the biblical text in order to make a particular point. Deuteronomy 34:1 is a valuable reference for the following quotations:

—In Thomas Hardy's *The Return of the Native*, Mrs. Yeobright is observed to have moments when "she seemed to be regarding issues from a Nebo denied to others around."
  a. What does Hardy want you to understand about Mrs. Yeobright?
  b. Is it vital to the story that the reader know the biblical reference?

—Elizabeth Barrett Browning's *Aurora Leigh* (1856) also refers to this verse in Deuteronomy in showing the essential difficulty of communicating with the contemporary audience. She asks if anyone

> "getting to the top of Pisgah-hill
> Can talk with one at bottom of the view,
> To make it comprehensible?"

a. How would you answer her question?

—One might describe people who read and study the Bible as those who have gotten "to the top of Pisgah-hill" and any unfamiliar with it as one at the "bottom of the view." Or is this the case only for reading older literature? Has anything been lost by the lack of general knowledge of the Bible? If there is a loss, is it literary only or also religious? Do people ever come to an interest in and study of the Bible—and to a religious relationship with it—through literature?

(M) Discuss this midrash.

● " 'And he was buried in the valley in the land of Moab over against Beth-peor' (Deut. 34:6). R[abbi] Berekhiah commented: Although Scripture thus provides one clue within another about its location, nevertheless [it goes on to say], 'No man knoweth of his sepulcher' (ibid.). The wicked kingdom of Rome once dispatched a request to the military garrison at Beth-peor: 'Locate the spot where Moses is buried.' When the soldiers stood on high ground, the spot seemed to them to be below; when they stood on low ground, it seemed to them to be above, fulfilling the words, 'No man knoweth of his sepulcher to this day' " (quoted in *The Book of Legends: Sefer Ha-Aggadah*, edited by Hayim Nahman Bialik and Yehoshua Hana Ravnitzky; Schocken Books, 1992; page 105).

(N) Reflect over this study.

● Ask class members to take a few minutes to think back over the entire study. After allowing them a few minutes for reflection, ask them to share their thoughts, perhaps even suggesting the following questions to think about:

—What was one surprising thing you learned about these books of the Bible?

—What was something special you learned about yourself?

—What questions have been raised in your mind?

—Is there something specific you have done as a result of any of these sessions?

● Unless the group's agenda is set in some other forum, you might also ask if there is anything growing out of this study that someone might like to do in the future.

Additional Bible Helps

This Writer's Musings About the Little Creed

Learning activity "F" has the class members compare the text of Deuteronomy 26:5-9 with the events that have taken place in the four biblical books studied this quarter. As soon as some scholars, beginning with Gerhard van Rad early in this century, isolated these verses and called them a "creed," other scholars noted that they made no mention of Sinai or of a covenant with God.

Many in the scholarly community took this to mean that there must have been at least two different groups of people—with two different traditions about God, the Lord—who came together and became the Israelites. One group knew of a covenant with a God who lived on a mountain. Another group believed their ancestors had been freed from slavery in Egypt. Somehow they all got together in the Promised Land and combined their stories until they became the Bible we now have.

I'm stating it too baldly, perhaps. Some of the arguments are quite technical and in all their technicality are often very compelling and persuasive. But I wonder sometimes if we forget about common sense when we delight in technical discoveries.

The Place of the Old Testament

Activity "G" has the class examine the Apostles' Creed, surely one of the most widely shared statements of basic Christian beliefs. Yet where in it is any mention of either Egypt or Sinai, covenant or Promised Land? Except for the one phrase "maker of heaven and earth" that can be connected to Genesis 1, there is nothing in the Apostles' Creed that explicitly mentions anything at all from the Old Testament.

Although there are a regrettable number of contemporary Christians who are "functional Marcionites," the church in its wisdom declared the second-century Marcion to be a heretic. (Among many other things, Marcion taught that Christians need not believe in the Old Testament because the Creator-God was not the same God as the Father of Jesus Christ.)

Even more important, Jesus clearly knew and taught from what we call the Old Testament. For Jesus, the disciples, and the early church, there was no such thing as an "Old" Testament. There was not yet any "New" Testament. It was simply Scripture, or "the Law and the Prophets."

"A wandering Aramean was my ancestor; he went down into Egypt and lived there as an alien, few in number, and there he became a great nation, mighty and populous" (Deuteronomy 26:5).

HELPS FOR THE LEADER

King James's English

This study has several times emphasized that we must be careful with word meanings if we are to understand the Scriptures. This is not only a matter of translation from one language to another; all living languages change. English has been no exception. Thus no translation, regardless of how accurate and beautiful it is when first completed, can serve endless generations.

The difficulty does not come so much with obsolete words. If you meet any of the following words, all you probably know about them is that you do not know them. You may skip over them; you may stop and look them up.

agone	hoise	ravin
astonied	knop	sith
chapiter	magnifical	taches
graff	marish	wot
habergeon	neezing	wotteth

Here are some other words that are likely to cause difficulty. They are still found today in the King James Version of the Bible (but with different meanings from the same words as used today).

You may find it somewhat easier to get these points across with a game.

● Prepare the first two columns of the following list ahead of time. Keep the third column blank. You may write the first two columns on the board or newsprint for everyone to use, or you may want to type it on paper and make copies for each team.

● The object of the game is to discover the present meaning of each word in column 1 in the verse where it appears in the 1611 (King James) version of the Bible.

● Assign each group some or all of the words in column one, along with the Bible passage where the word is found. Tell them to read the verse in a King James Bible and define the word as it is used there.

● Then, ask them to translate their word (or words) into modern English, giving the verse a different meaning.

● Take the first line, for example. Psalm 119:147 says "I prevented the dawning of the morning." In the modern use of words that would be quite an undertaking. A modern translation will say something on the order of "I got up before dawn," showing that "prevent" used to mean "go before" or "precede."

1	2	3
prevent	Psalm 119:147	preceded
let	Romans 1:13	prevented
demanded	Luke 3:14	asked
feebleminded	1 Thessalonians 5:14	faint-hearted
highminded	Romans 11:20	proud, haughty
all to brake	Judges 9:53	crushed
carelessly	Isaiah 47:8	free from care
compass	Joshua 6:3	march around
convert	Isaiah 6:10	turn
denounce	Deuteronomy 30:18	declare
dissolve doubts	Daniel 5:12	solve problems
imagination	Deuteronomy 29:19	stubbornness
comprehended	John 1:5	overcome
condescend	Romans 12:16	associate

● After groups have worked for a while, come back together and fill in column three with their definitions. See how close their words come to the suggested list. Some Bible translations use different terms than those chosen for this list.

● Class members may also want to take time to discuss a particular verse and its meaning. Perhaps some of these word changes will be new to them. Some people believe in seriousness and sincerity that when Jesus says "Suffer the little children" in Matthew 19:14 he means they are supposed to suffer. What was meant in Matthew 19:14 however is clear: "Allow the children to come" or "Let them come."

The Exodus in Literature and Music

I. Fictional treatments of themes from Exodus through Deuteronomy

Atwood, Margaret. *The Handmaid's Tale* (Fawcett, 1986; ISBN 0-449-21260-2). A novel about a most unpleasant future in which a horrific covenant theology built on a literalized Puritan model has resulted in a "theocracy" of terror.

Hurston, Zora Neale. *Moses, Man of the Mountain: A Novel* (HarperCollins, 1991; ISBN 0-06-091994-9, PL). A retelling of the Exodus story weaving together biblical materials with allusions to the social circumstances of African Americans in the United States in the 1930's. In some ways it is modern midrash, in that it fills in blanks in the biblical text with imaginative conjecture.

Steinbeck, John, *The Grapes of Wrath* (Viking Penguin, 1976; ISBN 0-14-004239-3) presents the Joads as modern Israelites fleeing through the desert from persecution toward the promised land of milk and honey in California, with Tom as their Moses. " 'Look,' he said, 'this ain't no lan' of milk an' honey like the preachers say . . .' " (chapter 20).

Uris, Leon, *Exodus* (Bantam, 1983; ISBN 0-553-25847-8). Telling the story of the re-establishment of Jews in Israel following the holocaust of World War II and attempting to remove much of the Western cultural typology from the story.

II. Other written works

Beegle, Dewey M., *God's Word into English* (Pryor Pettingill, 1965: ISBN 0-933462-02-6).

Bruce, F. F., *History of the Bible in English*, 3rd ed. (Oxford University Press, 1978; ISBN 0-19-520088-8).

Reumann, John H. P., *The Romance of Bible Scripts and Scholars* (Prentice Hall, 1965).

These three books concern several aspects of biblical transmission and translation. They are all more or less "popular" in style. Although relatively old, the first two are still in print, in paperback editions. The Reumann volume may be found in many church libraries.

Johnson, James Weldon. *God's Trombones: Seven Negro Sermons in Verse* (Viking Penguin, 1990; ISBN 0-14-018403-1). Not only the seven poem/sermons, but also Johnson's introductions are fascinating. The one on the Exodus ends:

"Listen!—Listen!
All you sons of Pharaoh.

Who do you think can hold God's people
When the Lord God himself has said,
Let my people go?" (page 52)

III. Music

Handel's oratorio, "Israel in Egypt" is great fun. It's much too long, of course, to listen to all of it during one regular session. Parts of it, though, should not be missed. In the short section on the plague of frogs they are so clearly jumping through the string section, you'll look under your chair to make sure you don't step on one.

Glossary of Terms

Anamnesis (an-am-NEE-sis)—Literally, "not forgetting," is a remembering with the entire self, putting oneself into the story.

Bemidbar (beh-mid-BAHR)—"In the wilderness," is the Hebrew name for the fourth book of the Bible, what we call Numbers.

Decalogue (DEK-uh-log)—The "Ten Words" or Ten Commandments. These are found both in Exodus 20 and Deuteronomy 5, with slight variations.

Devarim (de-vahr-EEM)—"The Words," the Hebrew name of the Book of Deuteronomy.

Henotheism (HEN-uh-thee-iz-uhm)—The belief that, regardless of whether or not there may be more than one god, you are supposed to worship and be loyal to only one.

Monotheism (MON-uh-thee-iz-uhm)—The belief that there is only one god.

Polytheism (POL-ee-thee-iz-uhm)—The belief that there is more than one god.

Shemot (sheh-MOHT)—"Names," the Hebrew name of the Book of Exodus.

Shema (shuh-MAH)—The first word of the passage in Deuteronomy 6, which begins "Hear, O Israel." The word itself means "Hear." It has come to be the name of the whole passage.

Tetragrammaton (tet-ruh-GRAM-uh-ton)—Literally, "four letters," refers to the sacred, four-letter, proper, personal name of God. Traditionally, it is never pronounced. Instead, one may substitute "LORD."

Torah (TOH-ruh)—a. The first five books of the Bible
b. Teaching, instruction
c. Law

Vayikra (vah-yik-RAH)—"And he called," the Hebrew name of the Book of Leviticus.

THE BIBLE IS…

By Dee Baker

Different people look at the Bible in different ways. Dr. Dorothy Jean Furnish has identified six perspectives from which Christians view the Bible.

What do *you* understand to be the nature and purpose of the Bible? To help you see the different ways people have been perceiving the Bible and to discover how your perceptions may vary from others, try this guided experience, either individually or with the class you are leading.

The following questionnaire, graph, and descriptions, based on Furnish's six perspectives, will help you clarify your thoughts and feelings about the Bible.

Questionnaire
Please respond to the following statements by circling the numbers of those with which you agree.

1. The Bible contains the Word of God.

2. Knowing about biblical history—dates, places, and events—increases our understanding of the biblical message.

3. The Bible is primarily a literary artifact that can teach us much about ancient places and times.

4. The Bible reveals struggles between God and persons.

5. The Word of God, the Bible, must speak without interpretation.

6. To understand the Bible, knowing about its authors, their audiences, and the cultural and historical settings in which biblical people lived is helpful.

7. Repeating the exact words of a Bible verse is an important way to learn the Word of God.

8. In order to get the meaning of a particular passage of the Bible, it is essential that the passage be seen in the context of that book of the Bible and the place of that book in the whole message of God.

9. By identifying with Bible characters, we may begin to understand our own feelings and responses to God's activity.

10. The Bible is the inspired and inerrant Word that God has passed on to his people.

11. Sociologists, anthropologists, and political scientists will find in the Bible valuable information about cultures, societies, and political systems.

12. Our response in faith to the Bible is what makes it the Word of God.

13. The Bible does not just tell us about events that have occurred, but it is an event in itself.

14. The Bible has value for Christians and non-Christians alike.

15. Knowing about biblical themes, teachings, events, and their meanings is more important than memorizing the exact words of Bible verses.

16. By understanding the history of the people in the Bible, we may come to understand God's action in our lives today.

17. The Bible is not only a book about God, but also a book about how people have encountered God.

18. The Bible contains moral and ethical guides and formulas for today's living.

19. The Bible reveals the history of God's people.

20. Entering dialogue with the characters of the Bible and trying to understand their feelings and experiences with God is helpful.

21. The Bible not only describes events where persons encountered God, but is itself a confronting event that can enable persons today to grow in their relationships with God.

22. The Bible not only contains information about the past, but also provides answers to problems of living today.

23. Learning Bible customs, geography, and sequences of events is important.

24. The writers of the Bible recorded God's literal word faithfully and accurately.

25. The Bible is an event through which God seeks to be known to us today.

26. The Bible is a book about human beings rather than about God.

27. The Bible offers a means by which we may see God's activity in our lives and a chance to respond to God's presence.

28. The King James Version of the Bible is the version that carries the authoritative words of God. Other translations are only interpretations that have tampered with the true Word.

29. The Bible tells of interactions that occur between God and creation.

30. In translating the Bible from Hebrew and Greek to Latin, and finally to English, exact meanings could not always be translated. Therefore, the understandings of the translators were interpreted into the text.

31. The historical accounts within the Bible are commentaries on God's revelation to God's people.

32. Before the Bible was put into written form, its lessons, stories, and poems were passed down from generation to generation by word of mouth. And in passing down traditions describing the nature of God different interpretations emerged.

33. The Bible was written by those who had witnessed encounters between God and humanity.

34. The Bible is a means by which we may encounter God.

35. In the biblical account we are reminded of all that God has done for God's people throughout history and into the present.

36. The Bible is the only source needed for faith.

Graph

Review your responses in the questionnaire. In the graph are numbers that correspond to the numbers of the statements you have read. After you have circled the numbers of the statements with which you agree, you are ready to circle the same numbers on the graph.

When you have finished marking the graph, look at the pattern of your responses. On which line do most of them appear? Is there any line where no responses appear?

WRITTEN & UNINTERPRETED	5	7	10	24	28	36
INTERPRETATION OF GOD'S WORD	1	6	8	15	30	32
SOURCE BOOK	3	11	14	18	22	26
HISTORY OF GOD'S PEOPLE	2	16	19	23	31	35
DIVINE-HUMAN ENCOUNTER	4	9	17	20	29	33
CONFRONTING EVENT	12	13	21	25	27	34

Many of these viewpoints are quite close to one another, and differ only in points of emphasis. Many people will find themselves agreeing with several different perspectives. That is all right. To better understand each perspective, consider the following ideas:

The Bible as God's Word Written and Uninterpreted
Most people who operate from this perspective understand the Bible's words in a literal way. No attempts at interpreting passages are acceptable; the text must speak for itself. In this perspective the Bible is seen as the actual, inerrant, literal Word of God. The writers of the Bible are considered to have been divinely inspired and to have recorded the actual words of God without error.

As such, the Bible is seen as self-explanatory, needing no aids, resources, or supplements for its understanding. The Bible is often considered the only source needed for faith. All portions of the Bible are considered to carry equal authority. Therefore, no sections or teachings of the Bible are stressed as more important than others.

Because of the high amount of faith invested in the Bible's literal words, memorization of Bible verses is seen as a central activity in education. It becomes very important for the exact words of a Bible passage to be repeated accurately. Some advocates of this approach are less literal than others, but it remains essential that the Bible be allowed to speak without interpretation.

The Bible as an Interpretation of God's Word

Methods of biblical research have led to better understandings of the cultural and historical settings of the Bible as well as the original Hebrew and Greek languages of the Bible. These findings have led many individuals to an understanding of the Bible as God's Word different from the perspective previously described.

Since our Bible began as stories and lessons passed orally from one generation to the next, passing down interpretations along with those stories was inevitable. Those who eventually wrote down their faith stories also allowed their interpretations of God's activity to come into the narrative. Similarly, once the Bible was translated into other languages, the interpretation of the translators affected the words chosen for the text.

In this perspective, the words of the Bible are not as important as understanding the themes and the meanings found within the Bible. The Bible contains the Word of God, but the Bible is not the Word of God in and of itself. Studying the context of a particular passage, knowing about the time, author, and reason for writing are essential to understanding God's word for us today.

The Bible as a Source Book

Some individuals view the Bible as useful to many people because of the historical and cultural data it contains. It is seen as an artifact, a collection of writings, some of which date back many centuries before Christ. Sociologists, anthropologists, historians, and political scientists would all have a special interest in relating the Bible to their fields of study.

Christians also use the Bible as a source book for their lives. Many see the Bible as a book containing prescriptions, or guides, for Christian ethical and moral behavior. Many solutions for everyday living are to be found in the Bible. As a guide for living today the Bible remains applicable.

The Bible as a History of God's People

The Bible is also described as a history of God's people. Like other histories, the Bible contains information about specific places and dates relating to the people of God. Its history is unique because it reveals the activity of God in people's lives.

Much attention is paid to recalling the great stories of faith—the Creation, the great Flood, the Exodus, the life, death, and Resurrection of Jesus Christ. Through this process Christians remember their heritage and the promise of God's activity in their lives.

The Bible as a Witness to Divine-Human Encounter

This perspective maintains the ideal that our relationship to God is not a passive but an active one. God's activity throughout history and in our lives demands a response on our part.

With this understanding, the Bible is seen as an account of God's activity in history. The Bible also serves as a history of humanity's responses to and encounters with God. Proponents maintain that the authors of the Bible were witnesses to such divine-human encounters.

In order to understand the importance of the Bible for us today, we need to enter dialogue with the characters found in the biblical record and try to understand their feelings, thoughts, and motivations. The biblical account then becomes real and applicable to our living encounters with God.

The Bible as a Confronting Event

Proponents of this perspective see the Bible as an event in the sense that God's active power and our encounter with that power can be precipitated by dialogue with the theme and meanings of the Bible.

In the sense that God's Word meets us through the biblical story and challenges us to respond, the Bible is seen as a confronting event. The Bible is one vital means by which we may come to experience God. And it is when we respond in faith to God's activity in the biblical story that the Bible truly becomes the word of God.

(Information in this article is based on *Exploring the Bible with Children*, by Dorothy Jean Furnish; Abingdon Press, 1978.)

Article adapted from "The Bible Is . . .," by Dee Baker; *Teacher* January 1991. Copyright © 1990 by Graded Press. Used by permission.